The Passion Christ fr Mystical City of God

By Mary of Agreda
Translated by Fiscar Morrison in 1902

Table of Contents

The Prayer of Our Lord in the Garden

The Prayer of Our Lord in the Garden and its Mysteries. What His most Blessed Mother knew of it.

By the wonderful mysteries, which our Savior Jesus had celebrated in the Cenacle, the reign which, according to his inscrutable decree, his eternal Father had consigned to Him, was well established; and the Thursday night of his last Supper having already advanced some hours, He chose to go forth to that dreadful battle of his suffering and death by which the Redemption was to be accomplished. The Lord then rose to depart from the hall of the miraculous feast and also most holy Mary left her retreat in order to meet Him on the way. At this face to face meeting of the Prince of eternity and of the Queen, a sword of sorrow pierced the heart of Son and Mother, inflicting a pang of grief beyond all human and angelic thought. The sorrowful Mother threw Herself at the feet of Jesus, adoring Him as her true God and Redeemer. The Lord, looking upon Her with a majesty divine and at the same time with the overflowing love of a Son, spoke to Her only these words: "My Mother, I shall be with thee in tribulation; let Us accomplish the will of the eternal Father and the salvation of men." The great Queen offered Herself as a sacrifice with her whole heart and asked his blessing. Having received this She returned to her retirement, where, by a special favor of the Lord, She was enabled to see all that passed in connection with her divine Son. Thus She was enabled to accompany Him and cooperate with Him in his activity as far as devolved upon Her. The owner of the house, who was present at this meeting, moved by a divine impulse, offered his house and all that it contained to the Mistress of heaven, asking Her to make use of all that was his during her stay in Jerusalem; and the Queen accepted his offer with humble thanks. The thousand angels of her guard, in forms visible to Her, together with some of the pious women of her company, remained with the Lady.

Our Redeemer and Master left the house of the Cenacle with all the men, who had been present at the celebration of the mysterious Supper; and soon many of them dispersed in the different streets in order to attend to their own affairs. Followed by his twelve Apostles, the Lord directed his steps toward mount Olivet outside and close to the eastern walls of Jerusalem. Judas, alert in his treacherous solicitude for the betrayal of his divine Master, conjectured that Jesus intended to pass the night in prayer as was his custom. This appeared to him a most opportune occasion for delivering his Master into the hands of his confederates, the scribes and the pharisees. Having taken this dire resolve, he lagged behind and permitted the 11aster and his Apostles to proceed. Unnoticed by the latter he lost them from view and departed in all haste to his own ruin and destruction. 'Within him was the turmoil of sudden fear and anxiety, interior witnesses of the wicked deed he was about to commit. Driven on in the stormy hurricane of thoughts raised by his bad conscience, he arrived breathless at the house of the high priests. On the way it happened, that Lucifer, perceiving the haste of Judas in procuring the death of Jesus Christ, and (as I have related in chapter the tenth), fearing that after all Jesl1, might be the true Messias, came toward him in the shape of a very wicked man, a friend of Judas acquainted with the intended betrayal. In this shape Lucifer could speak to Judas without being recognized. He tried to persuade him that this project of selling his Master did at first seem advisable on account of the wicked deeds attributed to Jesus; but that, having more maturely considered the matter, he did not now deem it advisable to deliver Him" over to the priests and pharisees; for Jesus was not so bad as Judas might imagine; nor did He deserve death; and besides He might free Himself by some miracles and involve his betrayer into great difficulties.

Thus Lucifer, seized by new fear, sought to counteract the suggestions with which he had previously filled the heart of the perfidious disciple against his Author. He hoped to confuse his victim; but his new villainy was in vain. For Judas, having voluntarily lost his faith and not being troubled by any such strong suspicions as Lucifer, preferred to take his Master's life rather than to encounter the wrath of the pharisees for permitting Him to live unmolested. Filled with this fear and his abominable avarice. he took no account of the counsel of Lucifer, although he had no suspicion of his not being the friend. whose shape the devil had assumed. Being stripped of grace he neither desired. nor could be persuaded by anyone. to turn back in his malice. The priests, having heard that the Author of life was in Jerusalem, had gathered to consult about the promised betrayal. Judas entered and told them that he had left his Master with the other disciples on their way to mount Olivet; that this seemed to be the most favorable occasion for his arrest, since on this night they had already made sufficient preparation and taken enough precaution to prevent his escaping their hands by his artifices and cunning tricks. The sacrilegious priests were much rejoiced and began to busy themselves to procure an armed force for the arrest of the most innocent Lamb.

In the meanwhile our divine Lord with the eleven Apostles was engaged in the work of our salvation and the salvation of those who were scheming his death. Unheard of and wonderful contest between the deepest malice of man and the unmeasurable goodness and charity of God! I f this stupendous struggle between good and evil began with the first man, it certainly reached its highest point in the death of the Repairer; for then good and evil stood face to face and exerted their highest powers: human malice in taking away the life and honor of the Creator and Redeemer, and his immense charity freely sacrificing both for men. According to our way of reasoning, it was as it were necessary that the most holy soul of Christ, yea that even his Divinity, should revert to his blessed Mother, in order that He might find some object in creation, in which his love should be recompensed and some excuse for disregarding the dictates of his justice. For in this Creature alone could He expect to see his Passion and Death bring forth full fruit; in her immeasurable holiness did his justice find some compensation for human malice; and in the humility and constant charity of this great Lady could be deposited the treasures of his merits, so that afterwards, as the new Phoenix from the rekindled ashes, his Church might arise from his sacrifice. The consolation which the humanity of Christ drew from the certainty of his blessed Mother's holiness gave Him strength and, as it were, new courage to conquer the malice of mortals; and He counted Himself well recompensed for suffering such atrocious pains by the fact that to mankind belonged also his most beloved Mother.

All that happened the great Lady observed from her retreat. She perceived the sinister thoughts of the obstinate Judas, how he separated himself from the rest of the Apostles, how Lucifer spoke to him in the shape of his acquaintance, and all the rest that passed when he reached the priests and helped them to arrange with so much haste the capture of the Lord. The sorrow which then penetrated the chaste heart of the Virgin Mother, the acts of virtue which She elicited at the sight of such wickedness, and what else She then did, cannot be properly explained by us; we can only say that in all She acted with the plenitude of wisdom and holiness, and with the approbation of the most holy Trinity. She pitied Judas and wept over the loss of that perfidious disciple. She sought to make recompense for his malice by adoring, confessing, praising and loving the Lord, whom he delivered by such fiendish and insulting treachery. She offered Herself with eagerness to die in her Son's stead, if necessary. She prayed for those who were plotting the capture and death of her divine Lamb, for She regarded them as prizes to be estimated according to the infinite value of his precious lifeblood for I which this most prudent Lady foresaw they would be bought.

Our Savior pursued his way across the torrent of Cedron (John 18, 1) to mount Olivet and entered the garden of Gethsemane. Then He said to all the Apostles: "Wait for Me, and seat yourselves here while I go a short distance from here to pray (Matthew 26, 36); do, you also pray, in order that you may not enter into temptation" (Luke 22, 40). The divine Master gave them this advice, in order that they might be firm in the temptations, of which He had spoken to them at the Supper: that all of them should be scandalized on account of what they should see Him suffer that night, that Satan would assail them to sift and stir them up by his false suggestions; for the Pastor (as prophesied) was to be illtreated and wounded and the sheep were to be dispersed (Zacharias 13, 7). Then the Master of life, leaving the band of eight Apostles at that place and taking with Him saint Peter, saint John, and saint James, retired to another place, where they could neither be seen nor heard by the rest (Mark 14, 33). Being with the three Apostles He raised his eyes up to the eternal Father confessing and praising Him as was his custom; while interiorly He prayed in fulfillment of the prophecy of Zacharias, permitting death to approach the most innocent of men and commanding the sword of divine justice to be unsheathed over the Shepherd and descend upon the God-man with all its deathly force. In this prayer Christ our Lord offered Himself anew to the eternal Father in satisfaction of his justice for the rescue of the human race; and He gave consent, that all the torments of his Passion and Death be let loose over that part of his human being, which was capable of suffering. From that moment He suspended and restrained whatever consolation or relief would otherwise overflow from the impassible to the passible part of his being, so that in this dereliction his passion and sufferings might reach the highest degree possible. The eternal Father granted these petitions and approved this total sacrifice of the sacred humanity.

This prayer was as it were the floodgate through which the rivers of his suffering were to find entrance like the resistless onslaught of the ocean, as was foretold by David (Psalms 68, 2). And immediately He began to be sorrowful and feel the anguish of his soul and therefore said to the Apostles: "My soul is sorrowful unto death" (Mark 14,34). As these words and the sorrow of Christ our Lord contain such great mysteries for our instruction, I will say something of what has been shown me and as far as I can understand concerning them. The Lord pennitted this sorrow to reach the highest degree both naturally and miraculously possible in his sacred humanity. This sorrow penetrated not only all the lower faculties of his human life in so far as his natural appetites were concerned; but also all the highest faculties of his lxxly and soul, by which He perceived the inscrutable judgments and decrees of the divine justice, and the reprobation of so many, for whom He was to die. This was indeed by far the greater source of his sorrow, as we shall see farther on. He did not say that He was sorrowful on account of his death, but. unto death; for the sorrow naturally arising from the repugnance to the death He was about to undergo, was a minor fear. The sacrifice of his natural life, besides being necessary for our Redemption, was also demanded as a return for the joy of having in his human body experienced the glory of the Transfiguration. On account of the glory then communicated to his sacred body He held Himself bound to subject it to suffering, deeming that a recompense of what He had received. This we see verified also in the three Apostles, who were witnesses as well of the glorious as of the sorrowful mystery. This they themselves now understood, being informed thereof by an especial enlightenment.

Moreover the immense love of our Savior for us demanded that full sway be given to this mysterious sorrow. For if He had caused it to stop short of the highest which that sorrow was capable of, his love would not have rested satisfied, nor would it have been so evident that his 100·e was not to be extinguished by the multitude of tribulations (Canticles 8, 7). At the same time He showed thereby his charity toward the Apostles, who were with Him and were now much disturbed by perceiving, that his hour of suffering and death, which He had so often and in so many ways foretold them. was now at hand. This interior disturbance and fear confounded and confused them without their daring to speak of it. Therefore the most loving Savior sought to put them more at rest by manifesting to them his own sorrow' unto death. By the sight of his own affliction and anxiety they were to take heart at the fears and anxieties of their own souls. There was still another mystery contained in this sorrow of the Lord, which referred especially to the three Apostles, saint Peter, John and James. For, more than all the rest, they were imbued with an exalted conception of the greatness and Divinity of their Master as far as the excellence of his doctrine, the holiness of his works, and the power of his miracles were concerned. They realized more completely and wondered more deeply at his dominion over all creation. In order that they might be confirmed in their belief of his being a man capable of suffering, it was befitting that they should know as eyewitnesses his truly human sorrow and affliction. By the testimony of these three Apostles who were distinguished by such favors, the holy Church was afterwards to be well fortified against the errors, which the devil would try to spread against the belief in the humanity of Christ our Savior. Thus would the rest of the faithful have the consolation of this firmly established belief in their own affliction and sorrow.

Interiorly enlightened in this truth, the three Apostles were exhorted by the Author of life by the words: "Wait for Me, watch and pray with Me." He wished to inculcate the practice of all that He had taught them and to make them constant in their belief. He thereby reminded them of the danger of backsliding and of the duty of watchfulness and prayer in order to recognize and resist the enemy, remaining always firm in the hope of seeing his name exalted after the ignominy of his Passion. With this exhortation the Lord separated Himself a short distance from the three Apostles. He threw himself with his divine face upon the ground and prayed to the eternal Father: "Father, if it is possible, let this chalice pass from ::'.le" (Matthew 26, 38). This prayer Christ our Lord uttered, though He had come down from heaven with the express purpose of really suffering and dying for men; though He had counteu as naught the shame of his Passion, had willingly emllraced it and rejected all human consolation; though He was hastening with most ardent love into the jaws of death, to affronts, sorrows and afflictions; though He had set such a high price upon men, that He determined to redeem them at the shedding of his lifeblood. ~ince by virtue of his divine and human wisdom and his inextinguishable love He had shown Himself so superior to the natural fear of death, that it seems this petition did not arise from any motive solely coming from Himself. That this was so in fact, was made known to me in the light which was vouchsafed me concerning the mysteries contained in this prayer of the Savior.

In order to explain what I mean, I must state, that on this occasion Jesus treated with the eternal Father about an affair, which was by far the most important of all, namely, in how far the Redemption gained by his Passion and Death should affect the hidden predestination of the saints. In this prayer Christ offered, on his part, to the eternal Father his torments, his precious blood and his Death for all men as an abundant price for all the mortals and for each one of the human born till that time and yet to be born to the end of the world; and. on the part of mankind. He presented the infidelity. ingratitude and contempt with which sinful man was to respond to his frightful

Passion and Death; He presented also the loss which He was to sustain from those who would not profit by his clemency and condemn themselves to eternal woe. Though to die for his friends and for the predestined was pleasing to Him and longingly desired by our Savior; yet to die for the reprobate was indeed bitter and painful; for with regard to them the impelling motive for accepting the pains of death was wanting. This sorrow was what the Lord called a chalice. for the Hebrews were accustomed to use this word for signifying anything that implied great labor and pain. The Savior himself had already used this word on another occasion. when in speaking to the sons of Zebedee He asked them: whether they could drink the chalice. which the Son of man was to drink (Matth 20. 22). This chalice then was so bitter for Christ our Lord. because He knew that his drinking it would not only be without fruit for the reprobate. but would be a scandal to them and redound to their greater ch::;.stisement and pain on account of their despising it (I Corinthians 1. 23).

I understood therefore that in this prayer. Christ besought his Father to let this chalice of dying for the reprobate pass from Him. Since now his Death was not to be evaded. He asked that none. if possible. should be lost; He pleaded. that as his Redemption would be superabundant for all. that therefore it should be applied to all in such a way as to make all. if possible, profit by it in an efficacious manner; and if this was not possible, He would resign Himself to the will of his eternal Father. Our Savior repeated this prayer three times at different intervals (Matthew 26, 44), pleading the longer in his agony in view of the importance and immensity of the object in question (Luke 22, 43). According to our way of understanding, there was a contention or altercation between the most sacred humanity and the Divinity of Christ. For this humanity, in its intense love for men who were of his own nature, desired that all should attain eternal salvation through his Passion; while his Divinity, in its secret and high judgments, had fixed the number of the predestined and in its divine equity could not concede its blessings to those who so much despised them, and who, of their own free will, made themselves unworthy of eternal life by repelling the kind intentions of Him who procured and offered it to them. From this conflict arose the agony of Christ, in which He prayed so long and in which He appealed so earnestly to the power and majesty of his omnipotent and eternal Father.

This agony of Christ our Savior grew in proportion to the greatness of his charity and the certainty of his knowledge, that men would persist in neglecting to profit by his Passion and Death (Luke

22, 44). His I agony increased to such an extent, that great drops of bloody sweat were pressed from Him, which flowed to the very earth. Although this prayer was uttered subject to a condition and failed in regard to the reprobate! who fell under this condition; yet He gained thereby a greater abundance and secured a greater frequency of favors for mortals. Through it the blessings were multiplied for those who placed no obstacles, the fruits of the Redemption were applied to the saints and to the just more abundantly, and many gifts and graces, of which the reprobates made themselves unworthy, were diverted to the elect. The human will of Christ, conforming itself to that of the Divinity, then accepted suffering for each respectively: for the reprobate, as sufficient to procure them the necessary help, if they would make use of its merits, and for the predestined, as an efficacious means, of which they would avail themselves to secure their salvation by cooperating with grace. Thus was set in order, and as it were realized, the salvation of the mystical body of his holy Church, of which Christ the Lord was the Creator and Head.

As a ratification of this divine decree, while yet our Master was in his agony, the eternal Father for the third time sent the archangel Michael to the earth in order to comfort Him by a sensible message and confirmation of what He already knew by the infused science of his most holy soul; for the angel could not tell our Lord anything He did not know, nor could he produce any additional effect on his interior consciousness for this purpose. But, as I related above, Christ had suspended the consolation, which He could have derived from his human nature from this knowledge and love, leaving it to its full capacity for suffering, as He afterwards also expressed Himself on the Cross. In lieu of this alleviation and comfort, which He had denied Himself, He was recompensed to a certain extent, as far as his human senses were concerned, by this embassy of the archangel. He received an experimental knowledge of what He had before known by interior consciousness; for the actual experience is something superadded and new and is calculated to move the sensible and bodily faculties. Saint Michael, in the name of the eternal Father, intimated and represented to Him in audible words, what He already knew, that it was not possible for those to be saved who were unwilling; that the complaisance of the eternal Father in the number of the just, although smaller than the number of the reprobate was great; that among the former was his most holy Mother, a worthy fruit of his Redemption; that his Redemption would also bear its fruits in the Patriarchs, Prophets, Apostles, Martyrs, Virgins and Confessors, who should signalize themselves in his love and perform admirable works for the exaltation of the name of the Most High. Among these the angel moreover mentioned some of the founders of religious orders and the deeds of each one. Many other great and hidden sacraments were touched upon by the archangel, which it is not necessary to mention here, nor have I any command to do so; and therefore what I have already said, will suffice for continuing the thread of this history.

During the intervals of Christ's prayer, the Evangelists say, He returned to visit the Apostles and exhort them to watch and pray lest they enter into temptation (Matthew 14,41; Mark 14,38; Luke 22, 42). This the most vigilant Pastor did in order to show the dignitaries of his Church what care and supervision they were to exercise over their flocks. For if Christ, on account of his solicitude for them interrupted his prayer, which was so important, it was in order to teach them, how they must postpone other enterprises and interests to the salvation of their subjects. In order to understand the need of the Apostles, I must mention, that the infernal dragon, after having been routed from the Cenacle and forced into the infernal caverns, was permitted by the Savior again to come forth, in order that he might, by his malicious attempts, help to fulfill the decrees of the Lord. At one fell swoop many of these demons rushed to meet Judas and, in the manner already described, to hinder him, if possible, from consummating the treacherous bargain. As they could not dissuade him, they turned their attention to the other Apostles, suspecting that they had received some great favor at the hands of the Lord in the Cenacle. What this favor was Lucifer sought to find out, in order to counteract it. Our Savior saw this cruelty and wrath of the prince of darkness and his ministers; therefore as a most loving Father and vigilant Superior He hastened to the assistance of his little children and newly acquired subjects, his Apostles. He roused them and exhorted them to watch and pray against their enemies, in order that they might not enter unawares and unprovided into the threatening temptation.

He returned therefore to the three Apostles, who, having been more favored, also had more reasons for watchfulness in imitation of their Master. But He found them asleep; for they had allowed themselves to be overcome by insidious disgust and sorrow and in it had been seized by such a remissness and lukewarmness, that they fell asleep. Before speaking to them or waking them, the Lord looked at them for a moment and wept over them. For He saw them oppressed and buried in this deathly shade by their own sloth and negligence. He spoke to Peter and said to him: "Simon, sleepest thou? couldst not thou watch one hour?" And immediately He gave him and the others the answer: "Watch ye, and pray that you enter not into temptation (Mark 14, 37); for my enemies and your enemies sleep not as you do." That He reprehended Peter especially was not only because he was placed as head of the rest, and not only because he had most loudly protested that he would not deny Him and was ready to die for Him, though all the others should be scandalized in Him and leave Him; but also because Peter, having from his whole heart made freely these protests, deserved to be corrected and admonished before all the rest. For no doubt the Lord chastises those whom He loves and is always pleased by our good resolutions, even when we afterwards fall short in their execution, as happened with the most fervent of all the Apostles, saint Peter. When the Lord came the third time and woke up all the twelve, Judas was already approaching in order to deliver Him into the hands of his enemies, as I shall relate in the next chapter.

Let us now return to the Cenacle, where the Queen of heaven had retired with the holy women of her company. From her retreat, by divine enlightenment, She saw most clearly all the mysteries and doings of her most holy Son in the garden. At the moment when the Savior separated Himself with the three Apostles Peter, John and James, the heavenly Queen separated Herself from the other women and went into another room. Upon leaving them She exhorted them to pray and watch lest they enter into temptation, but She took with Her the three Marys, treating Mary Magdalen as the superior of the rest. Secluding Herself with these three as her more intimate companions, She begged the eternal Father to suspend in Her all human alleviation and comfort, both in the sensitive and in the spiritual part of her being, so that nothing might hinder Her from suffering to the highest degree in union with her divine Son. She prayed that She might be permitted to feel and participate in her virginal body all the pains of the wounds and tortures about to be undergone by Jesus. This petition was granted by the blessed Trinity and the Mother in consequence suffered all the torments of her most holy Son in exact duplication, as I shall relate later. Although they were such, that, if the right hand of the Almighty had not preserved Her, they would have caused her death many times over; yet, on the other hand, these sufferings, inflicted by God himself, were like a pledge and a new lease of life. For in her most ardent love She would have considered it incomparably more painful to see her divine Son suffer and die without being allowed to share in his torments.

The three Marys were instructed by the Queen to accompany and assist Her in her affliction, and for this purpose they were endowed with greater light and grace than the other women. In retiring with them the most pure Mother began to feel unwonted sorrow and anguish and She said to them: "My soul is sorrowful, because my beloved Son is about to suffer and die, and it is not permitted me to suffer and die of his torments. Pray, my friends, in order that you may not be overcome by temptation." Having said this She went apart a short distance from them, and following the Lord in his supplications. She, as far as was possible to Her and as far as She knew it to be conformable to the human will of her Son, continued her prayers and petitions, feeling the same agony as that of the Savior in the garden. She also returned at the same intervals to her companions to exhort them, because She knew of the wrath of the demon against them. She wept at the perdition of the foreknown; for She was highly enlightened in the mysteries of eternal predestination and reprobation. In order to imitate and cooperate in all things with the Redeemer of the world, the great Lady also suffered a bloody sweat, similar to that of Jesus in the garden, and by divine intervention She was visited by the archangel saint Gabriel, as Christ her Son was visited by the archangel Michael. The holy prince expounded to Her the will of the Most High in the same manner as saint Michael had expounded it to Christ the Lord. In both of Them the prayer offered and the cause of sorrow was the same; and therefore They were also proportionally alike to one another in their actions and in their knowledge. I was made to understand that the most prudent Lady was provided with some cloths for what was to happen in the Passion of her most beloved Son; and on this occasion She sent some of her angels with a towel to the garden in which her Son was then perspiring blood, in order to wipe off and dry his venerable countenance. The Lord, for love of his Mother and for her greater merit, permitted these ministers of the Most High to fulfill her pious and tender wishes. When the moment for the capture of our Savior had arrived, it was announced to the three Marys by the sorrowful Mother. All three bewailed this indignity with most bitter tears, especially Mary Magdalen, who signalized herself in tenderest love and piety for her Master.

Instruction, which Mary, the Queen of Heaven Gave Me

My daughter, all that thou hast understood and written in this chapter will serve as a most potent incentive to thee and to all the mortals who will consider it carefully. Estimate then, and weigh within thy soul, how important is the eternal predestination or reprobation of the souls, since my most holy Son looked upon it with such great anxiety, that the difficulty or impossibility of saving all men added such immense bitterness to the Death, which He was about to suffer for all. By this conflict He manifests to us the importance and gravity of the matter under consideration, He prolonged his supplications and prayers to his eternal Father and his love for men caused his most precious blood to ooze forth from his body on perceiving, that the malice of men would make them unworthy of participation in the benefits of his Death. The Lord my Son has indeed justified his cause in thus having lavished his love and his merits without measure for the purchase of man's salvation; and likewise the eternal Father has justified Himself in presenting to the world such a remedy and in having made it possible for each one freely to reach out for such widely different lots, as death and life, fire and water (Ecclesiaticusls, 71).

But what pretense or excuse will men advance for having forgotten their own eternal salvation, when my divine Son and I have desired and sought to procure it for them with such sacrifices and untiring watchfulness? None of the mortals will have any excuse for their foolish negligence, and much less will the children of the holy Church have an excuse, since they have received the faith of these admirable sacraments and yet show in their lives little difference from that of infidels and pagans. Do not think, my daughter, that it is written in vain: "Many are called, but few are chosen" (Matthew 20, 16): fear this sentence and renew in thy heart the care and zeal for thy salvation, conformable to the sense of obligation arising from the knowledge of such high mysteries. Even if it were not a question of eternal salvation for thee, thou shouldst correspond to the loving kindness with which I manifest to thee such great and divine secrets. That I call thee my daughter and a spouse of my Lord, should cause thee to pay no attention to any visible thing and embrace only love and suffering for his sake. This I have shown thee by my example, since I applied all my faculties continually to these two things with the highest perfection. In order that thou mayest attain this, I wish that thy prayer be without intermission and that thou watch one hour with me, that is during the whole of thy life; for, compared with eternity, life is less than one hour, yea less than one moment. With such sentiments I wish that thou follow up the mysteries of the Passion, writing them, feeling them and imprinting them upon thy heart.

Our Savior Betrayed

Our Savior is delivered into the hands of his enemies by the treason of Judas and is taken prisoner; the behavior of the most holy Mary on this occasion and some of the mysteries of this event.

While our Savior occupied Himself in praying to his Father for the spiritual salvation of the human race, the perfidious disciple Judas sought to hasten thc delivery of Christ into the hands of the priests and pharisees. At the same time Lucifer and his demons, not being able to divert the perverse will of Judas and of the other enemies of Christ from their designs on the life of Christ their Creator and Master, changed the tactics of their satanic malice and began to incite the Jews to greater cruelty and effrontery in their dealings with the Savior. As I have already said several times, the devil was filled with great suspicions lest this most extraordinary Man bc the Messias and the true God. He now resolved to ascertain whether his misgivings were well founded or not by instigating the Jews and their ministers to the most atrocious injuries against the Savior. He imparted to them his own dreadful envy and pride, and thus literally fulfilled the prophecy of Solomon (Wisdom 2, 7). For it seemed to the demon, that if Christ was not God and only a man, He certainly must weaken and be conquered in these persecutions and torments. I f on the other hand He was God, He would manifest it by freeing Himself and performing new miracles.

Similar motives urged on the priests and pharisees. At the instigation of Judas they hastily gathered together a large band of people, composed of pagan soldiers, a tribune, and many Jews. Having consigned to them Judas as a hostage, they sent this band on its way to apprehend the most innocent Lamb, who was awaiting them and who was aware of all the thoughts and schemes of the sacrilegious priests, as foretold expressly by Jeremias (Jeremias 11, 19). All these servants of malice, bearing arms and provided with ropes and chains, in the glaring torch and lanternlight, issued from the city in the direction of mount Olivet. The prime mover of the treachery, Judas, had insisted upon so much precaution; for, in his perfidy and treachery, he feared that the meekest Master, whom he believed to be a magician and sorcerer, would perform some miracle for his escape. As if arms and human precautions could ever have availed if Jesus should have decided to make use of his divine power! As if He could not have brought this power into play in the same way as He had done on other occasions, should He now choose not to deliver Himself to suffering and to the ignominies of the Cross!

While they were approaching, the Lord returned the third time to his Apostles and finding them asleep spoke to them: "Sleep ye now, and take your rest. It is enough: the hour is come; behold the Son of man shall be betrayed into the hands of sinners. Rise up, let us go. Behold he that will betray Me is at hand" (Mark 14, 41). Such were the words of the Master of holiness to the three most privileged Apostles; He was unwilling to reprehend them more severely than in this most meek and loving manner. Being oppressed, they did not know what to answer their Lord, as Scripture says (Mark 14, 40). They arose and Jesus went with them to join the other eight disciples. He found them likewise overcome and oppressed by their great sorrow and fallen asleep. The Master then gave orders, that all of them together, mystically forming one body with Him their Head, should advance toward the enemies, thereby teaching them the power of mutual and perfect unity for overcoming the demons and their followers and for avoiding defeat by them. For a triple cord is hard to tear, as says Ecclesiastes (4, 12). and he that is mighty against one, may be overcome by two, that being the effect of union. The Lord again exhorted all the Apostles and forewarned them of what was to happen. Already the confused noise of the advancing band of soldiers and their helpmates began to be heard. Our Savior then proceeded to meet them on the way, and, with incomparable love, magnanimous courage and tender piety prayed interiorly: "O sufferings longingly desired

from my inmost soul, ye pains, wounds, affronts, labors, afflictions and ignominious death. come, come, come quickly, for the fire of love, which burns for the salvation of men, is anxious to see you meet the Innocent one of all creatures. Well do I know your value, I have sought, desired, and solicited you and I meet you joyously of my own free will; I have purchased you by my anxiety in searching for you and I esteem you for your merits. I desire to remedy and enhance your value and raise you to highest dignity. Let death come, in order that by my accepting it without having deserved it I may triumph over it and gain life for those who have been punished by death for their sins (Osee 13, 14). I give permission to my friends to forsake Me; for I alone desire and am able to enter into this battle and gain for them triumph and victory" (Isaias 53, 3).

During these words and prayers of the Author of life, Judas advanced in order to give the signal upon which he had agreed with his companions (Matthew 26, 48), namely the customary, but now feigned kiss of peace, by which they were to distinguish Jesus as the One whom they should single out from the rest and immediately seize. These precautions the unhappy disciple had taken, not only out of avarice for the money and hatred against his Master, but also, on account of the fear with which he was filled. For he dreaded the inevitable necessity of meeting Him and encountering IIim in the future, if Christ was not put to death on this occasion. Such a confusion he feared more than the death of his soul, or the death of his divine Master, and, in order to forestall it, he hastened to complete his treachery and desired to see the Author of life die at the hands of his enemies. The traitor then ran up to ~he meekest Lord, and, as a consummate hypocrite, hiding his hatred, he imprinted on his countenance the kiss of peace, saying: "God save Thee, Master." By this so treacherous act the perdition of Judas was matured and God was justified in withholding his grace and help. On the part of the unfaithful disciple, malice and temerity reached their highest degree; for, interiorly denying or disbelieving the uncreated and created wisdom by which Christ must know of his treason, and ignoring his power to destroy him, he sought to hide his malice under the cloak of the friendship of a true disciple; and all this for the purpose of delivering over to such a frightful and cruel death his Creator and Master, to whom he was bound by so many obligations. In this one act of treason he committed so many and such formidable sins, that it is impossible to fathom their immensity; for he was treacherous, murderous, sacrilegious, ungrateful, inhuman, disobedient, false, lying, impious and unequalled in hypocrisy; and all this was included in one and the same crime perpetrated against the person of God made man.

On the part of the Lord shone forth his ineffable mercy and equity, since those words of David were fulfilled in an eminent manner: "With them that hated peace I was peaceable; when I spoke to them they fought against Me without cause" (Psalms 119, 7). So completely did the Lord fulfill this prophecy, that when, in answer to the kiss of Judas, He said: "Friend, whereto art thou come?" He sent into the heart of the traitorous disciple a new and most clear light, by which Judas saw the atrocious malice of his treason, the punishment to follow, if he should not make it good by true penitence, and the merciful pardon still to be obtained from the divine clemency. What Judas clearly read in those few words of Christ was: "Friend, take heed lest thou cause thy perdition and abuse my meekness by this treason. If thou seek my friendship, I will not refuse it to thee on account of this deed, as soon as thou art sorry for thy sin. Consider well thy temerity in delivering Me by false friendship and under cover of a false peace and a kiss of reverence and love. Remember the benefits thou hast received of my charity, and that I am the Son of the Virgin, by whom thou hast been so often favored and rejoiced with motherly advice and counsel during thy apostolate. Even if it were only for her sake, thou shouldst not commit such a treason as to sell and deliver her Son. In no wise does her loving meekness deserve such an outrageous wrong, for She has never been unkind to thee. But although thou hast now committed this wrong, do not despise her intercession, for She alone will be powerful with Me and for her sake I offer thee pardon and life, since She has many times besought Me to do so. I assure thee, that We love thee; for thou art yet in life, where there is hope and where we will not deny thee our friendship, if thou seek it. But if thou refuse it, thou wilt merit our abhorrence and eternal chastisement and pain." The seed of the divine words took no root in the heart of that unhappy reprobate. It was harder than adamant and more inhuman than that of a wild beast. Resisting the divine clemency he finally fell into despair, as I shall relate in the next chapter.

The signal of the kiss having been given by Judas, the Lord with his disciples and the soldiers, who had come to capture Him, came face to face, forming two squadrons the most opposed and hosTHE that ever the world saw. For on the one side was Christ our Lord, true God and man, as the Captain of all the just, supported by his eleven Apostles the chieftains and champions of his Church with innumerable hosts of angelic spirits full of adoring wonder at this spectacle. On the other side were Judas, the originator of the treason, filled with hypocrisy and hatred, and many Jews and genTHEs, bent on venting their malice with the greatest cruelty. Surrounding these were Lucifer and a multitude of demons, inciting and assisting Judas and his helpers boldly to lay their sacrilegious hands upon their Creator. With unfathomable love for suffering and great force and authority the Lord then spoke to the soldiers, saying: "Whom seek ye?" (John 18,45). They answered: "Jesus of Nazareth." Jesus said to them: "I am He." By these inestimably precious and blessed words Christ declared Himself as our Redeemer and Savior; for only by his offering Himself freely to redeem us by his Passion and Death, could our hope of eternal life ever rest on firm foundation.

His enemies could not understand or fathom the true meaning of these words: I am He. But his most blessed Mother and the angels understood them, as did also, to a great extent, the Apostles. It was as if He had said: "I am who am" (Exodus 3, 14), as I have said to my prophet Moses; for I am of Myself, and all creatures have their being and existence from Me: I am eternal, immense, infinite, one in substance and attributes; and I have made Myself man hiding my glory, in order that, by means of my Passion and Death, to which you wish to condemn Me, I might save the world. As the Lord spoke with uivine power, his enemies could not resist and when his worus struck their ears, they all fell backwards to the ground (John 18, 6). This happened not only to the soldiers, but to the dogs, which they had brought with them, and to the horses on which some of them rode: all of them fell to the ground and remained motionless like stones. Luci fer anu his demons were hurled down with them, deprived of motion and suffering new confusion and torture. Thus they remained for some seven or eight minutes, showing no more signs of life than if they had died. O word of a God, so mysterious in meaning and more than invincible in power! Let not the wise glory before Thee in their wisdom and astuteness; nor the powerful in their valor (Jeremias 9, 23); let the vanity and arrogance of the children of Babylon be humbled, since one word from the mouth of the Lord, spoken with so much meekness and humility, confounds, destroys and annihilates all the pride and power of man and hell. Let us children of the Church also learn. that the victories of Christ are gained hy confessing the truth, by giving place unto wrath (Romans 12, 19), by showing meekness and humility of heart (1Iatth. 11, 29), by overcoming and being overcome with dove-like simplicity, by the peacefulness and resignment of sheep free from resistance of furious and ravenous wolves.

Sadly our divine Lord contemplated the picture of eternal damnation exhibited in them and listened to the prayer of his most holy Mother to let them rise, for upon her intercession his divine will had made that dependent. When it was time for them to come to themselves, He prayed to the eternal Father, saying: "My Father and eternal God, in my hands Thou hast placed all things (John 13, 3), and hast consigned to Me the Redemption required by thy justice. I wish to satisfy it and give Myself over to death with all my heart, in order to merit for my brethren participation in thy treasures and the eternal happiness held out to them." By this expression of his efficacious will the Lord gave permission to that whole miserable band of men, demons and animals to arise and be restored to the same condition as before their falling down. A second time the Savior said to them: "Whom seek ye?" and they again answered: "Jesus of Nazareth." The Lord answered most meekly: "I have already told you, that I am He. If therefore you seek Me, let these go their way" (John 18, 8). With these words He gave permission to the servants and the soldiers to take Him prisoner and execute their designs, which, without their understanding it, meant nothing else than to draw upon his divine Person all our sorrows and infirmities (Isaias 53, 4).

The first one who hastened to approach in order to lay hands upon the Master of life, was a servant of the high priests named Malchus. In spite of the fear and consternation of all the Apostles, saint Peter, more than all the rest, was roused with zeal for the defense of the honor and life of the divine Master. Drawing a cutlass which he had with him, he made a pass at Malchus and cut off one of his ears, severing it entirely from the head (John 18, 10). The stroke would have resulted in a much more serious wound, if the divine providence of the Master of patience and meekness had not diverted it. The Lord would not permit that any other death th:m his own should occur at his capture; his wounds, his blood and suffering alone should rescue to eternal life the human race, as many of it as are willing. Nor was it his will, or according to his teaching, that his Person be defended by the use of arms, and He did not wish to leave such an example in his Church as one to be principally imitated for her defense. In order to confirm this doctrine, which He had always inculcated, He picked up the severed ear and restored it to its place, perfectly healing the wound and making Malchus more sound and whole than he was before. But He first turned to saint Peter and reprehended him, saying: "Put up thy sword into the scabbard, for all that shall take it to kill with it, shall perish. Dost thou not wish that I drink the chalice, which my Father hath given Me? Thinkst thou that I cannot ask my Father, and He will give me presently many legions of angels for my defense? But how then shall the Scriptures and the Prophets be fulfilled?" (John 18, 11; Matthew 26, 53).

Thus saint Peter, the head of the Church, by this loving exhortation had been taught and enlightened, that his arms for the establishment and defense of the Church were to be spiritual and that the law of the Gospel does not inculcate battles and conquests with material weapons, but conquests of humility, patience, meekness and perfect charity, which overcome the demon, the world, and the flesh; that divine virtue would triumph over its enemies and over the power and intrigues of this world; that arms for attack and defense were not for the followers of Christ our Savior, but for the princes of the earth to safeguard their earthly possessions; while the sword of the Church was to be spiritual, reaching rather the soul than the body. Then Christ our Lord, turning toward his enemies and the servants of the Jews, spoke to them with great majesty and grandeur: "You are come as it were to a robber with swords and clubs to apprehend Me. I sat daily with you, teaching in the temple, and you laid not hands on Me. nut this is your hour and the power of darkness" (Matthew 26, 55; Luke 22, 53). All the words of our Savior contained the profoundest mysteries, and it is impossible to comprehend them all or explain them, especially those which He spoke at his Passion and Death.

Well might those ministers have been softened and made ashamed of their wickedness by this reprehension of the divine Master; but they were far from it, because they were of the cursed and sterile earth, drained of the dew of virtue and human kindness. Nevertheless the Author of life wished to admonish them of the truth to that extent. Thereby their malice would be so much the more inexcusable and this sin and all the others, committed in the very presence of the highest holiness and justice, would have its due correction and they themselves a powerful help for conversion, if they should desire it; moreover it would thereby become evident that He knew all that was to happen, that He delivered Himself into their hands and over to this Death of his own free will. For these, and for many other sublime reasons, the Lord spoke the above words. penetrating their inmost mind. For He knew and fully understood the cause of their malice, hatred and envy: namely, because He had publicly reprehended the vices of the priests and pharisees; because He had taught the truth and the way of life to the people; because He had, by his example and his miracles, captured the good will of the humble and the pious and brought many sinners to his friendship and grace. He reminded them, that one who had power to bring about all these results in public, and who could not be apprehended in the temple or in the city in which He taught, could certainly not be captured in the open field without his consent. He clearly made them sensible, that the reason of their failing to do so before, was because He himself had not given his permission to men or demons until the hour chosen by Himself. In order to signify to them, that the hour of his being captured, illtreated and afflicted had come He said: "This is your hour and the power of darkness." As if He had said to them: Until now it was necessary for Me to be with you as your Master for your instruction, therefore I did not permit you to take my life. But I desire to consummate by my death the work of the Redemption consigned to Me by my eternal Father; and therefore I now permit you to take Me prisoner and to execute your will upon my Person. Thereupon they fell upon the most meek Lamb like fierce tigers, binding Him securely with ropes and chains in order thus to lead Him to the house of the high priest, as I shall presently relate.

The most pure Mother of Christ our Lord was most attentive to all that passed in his capture, and by means of her clear visions saw it more clearly than if She had been present in person; for by means of her supernatural visions She penetrated into all the mysteries of his words and actions. When She beheld the band of soldiers and servants issuing from the house of the high priest, the prudent Lady foresaw the irreverence and insults with which they would treat their Creator and Redeemer; and in order to do what was within her power, She invited the holy angels and many others in union with Her to render adoration and praise to the Lord of creation as an offset to the injuries and affronts He would sustain at the hands of those ministers of darkness. The same request She made to the holy women who were praying with Her. She told them, that her most holy Son had now given permission to his enemies to take him prisoner and illtreat him, and that they were about to make use of this permission in a most impious and cruel manner. Assisted by the holy angels and the pious women the faithful Queen engaged in interior and exterior acts of devoted faith and love, confessing, adoring, praising and magnifying the infinite Deity and the most holy humanity of her Creator and Lord. The holy women imitated Her in the genuflections and prostrations, and the angelic princes responded to the canticles with which She magnified, celebrated and glorified the Divinity and humanity of Christ. In the measure in which the children of malice increased their irreverence and injuries, She sought to compensate them by her praise and veneration. Thus She continued to placate the divine justice, lest it should be roused against his persecutors and destroy them; for only most holy Mary was capable of staying the punishment of such great offenses.

And the great Lady not only placated the just Judge, but even obtained favors and blessings from the divine clemency for the very persons who irritated Him and thus secured a return of good for those who were heaping wrongs upon Christ the Lord for his doctrine and benefits. This mercy attained its highest point in the disloyal and obstinate Judas; for the tender Mother, seeing him deliver Jesus by the kiss of feigned friendship, and considering how shortly before his mouth had contained the sacramental body of the Lord, with whose sacred countenance so soon after those same foul lips were permitted to come in contact, was transfixed with sorrow and entranced by charity. She asked the Lord to grant new graces, whereby this man, who had enjoyed the privilege of touching the face whereon angels desire to look, might, if he chose to use them, save himself from perdition. In response to this prayer of most holy Mary, her Son and Lord granted Judas powerful graces in the very consummation of his treacherous delivery. If the unfortunate man had given heed and had commenced to respond to them, the Mother of mercy would have obtained for him many others and at last also pardon for his sin. She has done so with many other great sinners, who were willing to give that glory to Her, and thus obtain eternal glory for themselves. But Judas failed to realize this and thus lost all chance of salvation, as I shall relate in the next chapter.

Likewise, when the great Lady saw all the servants and soldiers who had come to take Him, fall to the ground at his divine word, She, in company with the angels, broke out in a song of praise of his infinite power and of the virtue of his humanity, which thereby renewed the victory of the Most High over Pharao and his troops in the Red sea (Exodus 15,4). She exalted the Lord of hosts, because He was about to deliver Himself in an admirable manner to suffering and death in order to save the human race from the captivity of Lucifer. Then She besought the Lord to permit all these dumbfounded and vanquished enemies to regain their senses and to arise. She was moved to the petition by her most generous kindness and deep compassion for these men created by the Lord according to his own image and likeness; on the other hand, She wanted to fulfill in an eminent degree the law of loving our enemies and doing good to those who persecute us, inculcated and practiced by her own Son and Master (Matthew 5, 44), and finally because She knew that the prophecies of holy Scripture were to be fulfilled in the Redemption of man. Although all these were infallible, this did not hinder the most holy Mary from giving voice to her prayer and thereby moving the Most High to grant these favors; for in the infinite wisdom and in the decrees of his eternal will all these means were foreseen as producing these effects in the manner most conformable to the foreknowledge and foresight of the Lord. But it is not necessary to enter into further explanation of such mysteries at present. When the servants of the high priest laid hands on and bound the Savior, the most blessed Mother felt on her own hands the pains caused by the ropes and chains, as if She Herself was being bound and fettered; in the same manner She felt in her body the blows and torments further inflicted upon the Lord, for, I have already said, this favor was granted to his Mother, as we shall see in the course of the Passion. This her sensible participation in his sufferings was some kind of relief of the pain, which She would have suffered in her loving soul at the thought of not being with Him in his torments.

Instruction, which Mary, the Queen of Heaven Gave Me

My daughter, in all that thou art made to understand and write concerning these mysteries, thou drawest upon thyself (and upon mortals) a severe judgment, if thou dost not overcome thy pusillanimity, ingratitude and baseness by meditating day and night on the Passion and Death of Jesus crucified. This is the great science of the saints, so little heeded by the worldly; it is the bread of life and the spiritual food of the little ones, which gives wisdom to them and the want of which starves the lovers of this proud world (Wisdom IS, 3). In this science I wish thee to be studious and wise, for with it thou canst buy thyself all good things (Wisdom 7, 11). My Son and Lord taught us this science when He said: "I am the way, the truth and the life: no one cometh to my Father except through Me" (John 14, 6). Tell me then, my daughter: if my Lord and Master has made Himself the life and the way for men through his Passion and Death, is it not evident that in order to go that way and live up to this truth, they must follow Christ crucified, afflicted, scourged and affronted? Consider the ignorance of men who wish'to come to the Father without following Christ, since they expect to reign with God without suffering or imitating his Passion, yea without even a thought of accepting any part of his suffering and Death, or of thanking Him for it. They want it to procure for them the pleasures of this life as well as of eternal life, while Christ their Creator has suffered the most bitter pains and torments in order to enter heaven and to show them by his example how they are to find the way of light,

Eternal rest is incompatible with the shame of not having duly labored for its attainment. He is not a true son of his father, who does not imitate him, nor he a good disciple, who does not follow his Master, nor he a good servant, who does not accompany his lord; nor do I count him a devoted child, who does not suffer with me and my uivine Son. But our love for the eternal salvation of men obliges us, who see them forgetful of this truth and so adverse to suffering, to send them labors and punishments, so that if they do not freely welcome them, they may at least be forced to undergo them and so be enabled to enter upon the way of salvation. And yet even all this is insufficient, since their inclinations and their blind love of visible things detains them and makes them hard and heavy of heart; they rob them of remembrance and affection toward these higher things, which might raise them above themselves and above created things. Hence it comes, that men do not find joy in their tribulations, nor rest in their labors, nor consolation in their sorrows, nor any peace in adversities. For, altogether different from the saints who glory in tribulation as the fulfillment of their most earnest desires, they desire none of it and abhor all that is painful. In many of the faithful this ignorance goes still farther; for some of them expect to be distinguished by God's most intimate love, others, to be pardoned without penance, others, to be highly favored. Nothing of all this will they attain, because they do not ask in the name of Christ the Lord and because they do not wish to imitate Him and follow Him in his Passion.

Therefore, my daughter, embrace the Cross and do not admit any consolation outside of it in this mortal life. By contemplating and feeling within thyself the sacred Passion thou wilt attain the summit of perfection and attain the love of a spouse. Bless and magnify my most holy Son for the love with which He delivered Himself up for the salvation of mankind. Little do mortals heed this mystery; but I, as an Eyewitness, assure thee, next to ascending to the right hand of his eternal Father, nothing was so highly estimated and so earnestly desired by Him, as to offer Himself for suffering and death and to deliver Himself up entirely to his enemies. I wish also that thou lament with great sorrow the fact that Judas, in his malice and treachery, has many more followers than Christ. Many are the infidels, many the bad Catholics, many the hypocrites, who under the name of a Christian, sell and deliver Him and wish to crucify Him anew. Bewail all these evils, which thou understand est and knowest, in order that thou mayest imitate and follow me in this matter.

The Flight of the Apostles

The flight and dispersion of the Apostles after the capture of their master; how his most blessed mother was aware of all that happened and how she acted in consequence; the perdition of Judas and the worry of the demons over what they were obliged to experience.

After the seizure of our Savior Jesus, his prophecy at the Supper, that all of the Apostles would be greatly scandalized in his Person (Matthew 26, 31) and that satan would attack them in order to sift them like wheat, was fulfilled. For when they saw their divine Master taken prisoner and when they perceived, that neither his meekness, nor his words so full of sweetness and power, nor his miracles, nor his doctrine exemplified by such an unblamable life, could appease the envy of the priests and pharisees, they ·fell into great trouble and affliction. Naturally the fear of personal danger diminished their courage and confidence in the counsels of their Master, and beginning to wander in their faith, each one became possessed with anxious thoughts as to how he could escape the threatening persecutions foreshadowed by what had happened to their Captain and Master. The Apostles, availing themselve~ of the preoccupation of the soldiers and servants in binding and fettering the meek Lamb of God, betook themselves to flight unnoticed. Certainly their enemies, if they had been permitted by the Author of life, would have captured all the Apostles, especially if they had seen them fly like cowards or criminals (Matthew 26, 56). But it was not proper that they should be taken and made to suffer at that time. This was clearly indicated as the will of the Lord, when He said: that if they sought Him, they should let his companions go free; these words had the force of a divine decree and were verified in the event. For the hatred of the priests and pharisees extended to the Apostles, and was deep enough to make them desire the death of all of them. That is the reason why the high priest Annas asked the divine Master about his disciples and his doctrine (John 18,8).

At the flight of the Apostles, Lucifer, already troubled and vaguely perplexed, betook himself off hesitating between different projects of his redoubled malice. He certainly wished to see the doctrine of the Savior and all his disciples blotted out from the world, so that not even the memory of them be left. Hence he would have been well satisfied, if the Jews had imprisoned and killed them all. But he had no hope of easily attaining this wish, and therefore he busied himself in disquieting the Apostles by various suggestions and inciting them to flight, in order that they might not witness the patience and virtues of their IIaster in his sufferings. The astute dragon feared, that by this new proof of his doctrine in his living example the Apostles might be confirmed and fortified in their faith and thus resist the temptations which he planned for them; therefore it seemed to him, that if he could weaken them now, he could more easily cause them to fall away entirely by subsequent persecutions easily to be raised against them among the only too ready enemies of their Master. Thus the demon c\eceived himself by his own malicious calculations. When therefore he saw the Apostles filled with cowardly fear and much disturbed by the sorrow of their hearts, he rejoiced in their evil plight and considered it the best time to begin his temptations. He assailed them with rabid fury, filling them with strong doubts and suspicions against the Master of life and urging them to give Him up and betake themselves to flight. They easily yielded to his suggestions of flight; but they resisted many of the doubts against faith, although some failed more, some less, not all of the Apostles being equally disturbed or scandalized.

They separated from each other, scattering in different directions; for it would have been difficult for all of them to hide as they wished, if they remained together. Only saint Peter and saint John kept each other company to follow their God and Master and see the end of his misfortune (Matthew 26, 58). But in the soul of each one of the eleven Apostles raged a battle of sorrow and grief, which wrung their hearts and left them without consolation or the least rest. On the one side battled reason, grace, faith, love and truth; on the other temptation, suspicion, fear, cowardice and sorrow. Reason and truth reproached them with their inconstancy and disloyalty in having forsaken their Master by cowardly flying from danger, after having been warned of it and after having offered themselves so shortly before to die for Him if necessary. They remembered their disobedience in neglecting to pray and strengthen themselves against temptations, as the Lord had commanded them. Their love for his sweet conversation and company, for his teaching and miraculous power, and their conviction that He was true God, urged them to return and seek Him, and to offer themselves to danger and death like faithful servants and disciples. To all this was joined the memory of his most sweet Mother, the consideration of her intense sorrow, and the desire to seek Her and attend upon Her in her trouble. But on the other hand was their timidity, exaggerating their fears of the Jews, their dread of death, of shame and confusion. In regard to seeking the company of the sorrowful Mother, they feared lest She would oblige them to return to their Master, and lest they should be more easily found if they stayed with Her in the same house. Dreadful above all were the impious and horrible suggestions of the demons. For the dragon filled them with harassing doubts, whether it would not be suicide to thus deliver themselves to a certain death; that, if their Master could not free Himself, much less could He free them from the hands of the priests; that He would now certainly be put to death, and that therefore all ties between Him and them were dissolved, since they would not see Him any more; that, although his life seemed to be blameless, yet He had taught some very hard doctrines, some of them unheard of until that time, whence He had incurred the hatred of those learned in the law and of the priests, as well as the indignation of all the people. Moreover it was a serious matter to follow a Man, who was to be condemned to an infamous and frightful death.

Such was the interior contention and strife in the hearts of the Apostles. Satan under cover of this excitement, continually sought to instill into their minds doubts concerning the teachings of Christ and concerning the prophecies, that treated of the mysteries of his Passion. As in their sad interior conflict they failed to see the least assurance of seeing their Master escape the hands of the priests alive, their fears settled into a profound sorrow and melancholy, in which they decided to fly from the danger and save their own lives. And they were seized with such timidity and cowardice, that during this night they felt nowhere safe, and every shadow or noise made them tremble with fear. The consideration of the treachery of Judas added still more to their fear; for, as he had not been seen in the company of any of the eleven after his treacherous delivery of the Lord, they dreaded lest he should excite against them the hatred of the priests. Saint Peter and saint John, being more fervent in the love of their Master, made a greater show of resistance to fear and to the demon; and the two together resolved to follow their Master at a distance. In taking this resolve, they relied much upon the acquaintance of saint John with the high priest Annas, who with Caiphas alternated in the office of high priest. In that year it was held by Caiphas, who in the meeting had given the prophetic counsel, asking whether one man had not better die in order that the whole world might not perish (John 18, 15, 49). This acquaintance had arisen from the fact, that saint John was esteemed as a man, distinguished and of noble lineage, of affable and courteous manners and amiable in person. Trusting to these favorable circumstances the two Apostles followed the Lord with less fear. The thought of their heavenly Queen was deep in their hearts, and they reflected on her bitter sorrow and desired to bring relief and console Her if possible. In this pious and loving desire especially saint John excelled all the others.

The heavenly Princess, from the Cenacle, clearly understood and saw all: not only her most holy Son in captivity and suffering, but all that happened inwardly and outwardly to the Apostles. She observed their tribulation and temptations, their thoughts and resolves, where each one was and what he did. But although as was known to the most gentle Dove, She allowed Herself no feeling of indignation against the Apostles, nor did She ever in the least reproach them for their disloyalty; on the contrary, She was the One, who was principally instrumental in restoring them to a better mind, as I shaH show later on (746, 747). From that hour on She commenced to pray for them. In sweetest charity and with the compassion of a Mother, She interiorly addressed them: "O ye simple sheep, chosen by the Lord, do ye forsake your most loving Pastor, who cares for you and feeds you on the pastures of eternal life? Why, being disciples of such a truthful doctrine, do you leave your Benefactor and Master? How can you forget the sweet and loving intercourse, which so attracted your hearts? Why do you listen to the master of lies and follow the ravenous wolf, who seeks your ruin? O most patient and sweetest Lord, how meek, and kind and merciful does the love of men make Thee! Extend thy gentle love to this little flock. which is now troubled and dispersed by the fury of the serpent. Do not deliver over to the beasts those souls, who have confessed thy name (Psalms 73, 19). Great hopes hast thou set in those, whom Thou hast chosen as thy servants and through whom Thou hast already accomplished great things. Let not such graces be in vain, nor reject those whom Thou hast freely chosen for the foundations of thy Church. Let not Lucifer glory in having, beneath thy very eyes, vanquished the best of thy family and household. My Son and Lord, look upon thy beloved disciples John, Peter and James, so much favored by thy love and good will. Turn an eye of clemency also upon the rest, crush the pride of the dragon, which now pursues them with implacable fury."

In all that most holy Mary did on this occasion and in the pleasure She caused the Almighty by her holiness, She exceeded in grandeur all that was ever possible in men and angels. Over and above the sensible and spiritual sorrows caused by the torments of her divine

Son and the affronts perpetrated against his divine Person (for which the blessed Mother entertained the highest veneration attainable by a creature), She was overwhelmed with the sorrow caused by the fall of the Apostles, the greatness of which She alone could properly estimate. She was obliged to witness their weakness and forgetfulness in the face of his divine favors, his doctrines and exhortations, and in so short a time after the last Supper, when He had warned them so lovingly, given them holy Communion and elevated them to such a high dignity as the priesthood. She saw also the danger of their falling into even greater sins on account of the astute and furious attacks of Lucifer and his demons, and on account of the heedlessness of the Apostles in their greater or less confusion and fear. Yet notwithstanding this great sea of sorrow She multiplied and intensified her petitions in order to merit for them sufficient assistance and speedy pardon from her Son, so that they might again return to their faith and to his friendship in grace. She alone was the powerful and efficacious instrument of these results. During these hours the great Lady united within Herself all the faith, all the holiness, all the worship and divine cult of the Church; for in Her was preserved and enclosed as in the living and incorruptible ark and as in the temple and sanctuary, the evangelical law and sacrifice. She by Herself alone then constituted the entire Church, because She alone preserved full faith, hope and love, complete worship and adoration for the great object of our faith, not only supplying her full share for Herself, but for the Apostles and for the whole human race. She it was who compensated, as far as was possible to a creature, for the deficiencies and faults in the rest of the mystical members of the Church. She performed heroic acts of faith, hope, love toward Her Son and true God, She venerated and adored Him by her prostrations and genuflections, She blessed Him with wonderful songs of praise, not allowing her deep and bitter sorrow to interfere with the beautiful and harmonious disposition and the full operation of all her faculties, as preordained by the Almighty. What Ecclesiasticus says of music: that it is inopportune in time of sorrow (Ecclesiaticus 22, 6), does not apply to Her; for only the blessed Mary was able and knew how to augment the beautiful harmony of virtues in the midst of sorrow.

Leaving the twelve Apostles in the sad state above mentioned, I now proceed to relate the mogt unhappy end of the traitor Judas, somewhat anticipating the course of events, in order to have done with his lamentable and unfortunate lot and continue the narrative of the Passion. With the band that had taken the Lord prisoner, the sacrilegious disciple arrived at the house of the high priest, that of Annas first, and then at that of Caiphas, who, with the scribes and pharisees were awaiting results. When the perfidious disciple saw his divine Master overwhelmed with blasphemies and injuries and how He suffered all with such admirable silence, meekness and patience, he began to reflect upon his own treachery and that it alone caused such cruel injustice to be heaped upon an innocent Man and his Benefactor. He recalled the miracles he had witnessed, the doctrines he had heard, and the benefits enjoyed at his hands, and he remembered the kindness and meekness of the most holy Mary, the charity with which She had solicited his conversion, and the malice with which he had offended the Son and the Mother for such insignificant gain. All the sins he had committed piled themselves up before his interior gaze like a dark and chaotic, impenetrable mountain.

As I have stated above, Judas was forsaken by divine grace at the time when he consummated his treachery by his perfidious kiss and by his contact with Christ our Savior. According to the hidden judgments of the Most High, although he was now left to his own counsels, the divine justice and equity, ingrained in the natural reason, permitted these reflections to arise and to be supplemented by many suggestions of Lucifer who possessed him. But though Judas thus reasoned correctly in these matters, it was the devil who awakened these truths and added many other false and deceitful suggestions, in order to deduct from them not the salutary hope of remedy, but to convince him of the impossibility of repairing the damage and to lead him to the despair to which he at last yielded. Lucifer roused in him a keen sorrow for his misdeeds; not however for a good purpose, nor founded upon having offended the divine Truth, but upon his disgrace among men and upon the fear of retribution from his Master, whom he knew to be miraculously powerful and One whom he would be able to escape nowhere in the whole world. Everywhere the blood of the just One would forever cry for vengeance against him. Filled with these thoughts and others aroused by the demon, he was involved in confusion, darkness and rabid rage against himself. Fleeing from all human beings he essayed to throw himself from the highest roof of the priests' house without being able to execute his design. Gnawing like a wild beast at the flesh of his arms and hands, striking fearful blows at his head, tearing out his hair and raving in his talk, he rushed away and showered maledictions and execrations upon himself as the most unfortunate and miserable of men.

Seeing him thus beside himself Lucifer inspired him with the thought of hunting up the priests, returning to them the money and confessing his sin. This Judas hastened to do, and he loudly shouted at them those words: "I have sinned, betraying innocent blood!" (Matthew 27, 4). But they, not less hardened, answered that he should have seen to that before. The intention of the demon was to hinder the death of Christ if possible, for reasons already given and yet to be given. This repulse of the priests, so full of impious cruelty, took away all hope from Judas and he persuaded himself that it was impossible to hinder the death of his Master. So thought also the demon, although later on he made more efforts to forestall it through Pilate. But as Judas could be of no more use to him for his purpose, he augmented his distress and despair, persuading him that in order to avoid severer punishments he must end his life. Judas yielded to this terrible deceit, and rushing forth from the city, hung himself on a dried out fig tree (Matthew 27, 5). Thus he that was the murderer of his Creator, became also his own murderer. This happened on Friday at twelve o'clock. three hours before our Savior died. It was not becoming that his death and the consummation of our Redemption should coincide too closely with the execrable end of the traitorous disciple, who hated him with fiercest malice.

The demons at once took possession of the soul of Judas and brought it down to hell. His entrails burst from the body hanging upon the tree (Acts 1, 18). All that saw this stupendous punishment of the perfidious and malicious disciple for his treason, were filled with astonishment and dread. The body remained hanging by the neck for three days, exposed to the view of the public. During that time the Jews attempted to take it down from the tree and to bury it in secret, for it was a sight apt to cause great confusion to the pharisees and priests, who could not refute such a testimony of his wickedness. But no efforts of theirs sufficed to drag or separate the body from its position on the tree until three days had passed, when, according to the dispensation of divine justice, the demons themselves snatched the body from the tree and brought it to his soul, in order that both might suffer eternal punishment in the profoundest abyss of hell. Since what I have been made to know of the pains and chastisements of Judas, is worthy of fearinspiring attention, I will according to command reveal what has been shown me concerning it. Among the obscure caverns of the infernal prisons was a very large one, arranged for more horrible chastisements than the others, and which was still unoccupied; for the demons had been unable to cast any soul into it, although their cruelty had induced them to attempt it many times from the time of Cain unto that day. All hell had remained astonished at the failure of these attempts, being entirely ignorant of the mystery, until the arrival of the soul of Judas, which they readily succeeded in hurling and burying in this prison never before occupied by any of the damned. The secret of it was, that this cavern of greater torments and fiercer fires of hell, from the creation of the world, had been destined for those, who, after having received Baptism, would damn themselves by the neglect of the Sacraments, the doctrines, the Passion and Death of the Savior, and the intercession of his most holy Mother. As Judas had been the first one who had so signally participated in these blessings, and as he had so fearfully misused them, he was also the first to suffer the torments of this place, prepared for him and his imitators and followers.

This mystery I was commanded to reveal more particularly for a dreadful warning to all Christians, and especially to the priests, prelates and religious, who are accustomed to treat with more familiarity the body and blood of Christ our Lord, and who, by their office and state are his closer friends. In order to avoid blame I would like to find words and expressions sufficiently strong to make an impression on our unfeeling obduracy, so that we all may take a salutary warning and be filled with the fear of the punishments awaiting all bad Christians according to the station each one of us occupies. The demons torment Judas with inexpressible cruelty, because he persisted in the betrayal of his Master, by whose Passion and Death they were vanquished and despoiled of the possession of the world. The wrath which they had conceived against the Savior and his blessed Mother, they wreck, as far as is allowed them, on all those who imitate the traitorous disciple and who follow him in his contempt of the evangelical law, of the Sacraments and of the fruits of the Redemption. And in this the demons are but executing just punishment on those members of the mystical body of Christ, who have severed their connection with its head Christ, and who have voluntarily drifted away and delivered themselves over to the accursed hate and implacable fury of his enemies. As the instruments of divine justice they chastise the redeemed for their ingratitude toward their Redeemer. Let the children of the Church consider well this truth, for it cannot fail to move their hearts and induce them to evade such a lamentable fate.

During the whole course of the Passion Lucifer with his demons moved about, eagerly spying out all the circumstances of each event in order to ascertain whether Christ the Lord was really the Messias and Redeemer of the world. On the one hand the miracles seemed to argue the truth of his suspicions, on the other very often the doings and the. sufferings, so much like those of weak human nature, argued the contrary. The strongest argument for the truth of his suspicions was Lucifer's personal experience of the power of the Redeemer, when He said "I am He," which caused him and all his associates to fall prostrate, annihilated in the presence of the Lord; and this had happened only a short time after he had been permitted to issue from hell, whither the demons had been hurled from the Cenacle. It was true, Mary had routed them from the hall of the last Supper; yet Lucifer with his ministers connected it with the power exercised by Jesus and they could not but admit, that this power of both Mother and Son as something altogether new and unexperienced by them. When he had received permission to rise from his fall in the garden, he conferred with the rest and expressed his opinion, that this could not be merely human power, but without doubt the power of One, who is God and at the same time man. "If He shall die, as we have planned, He will accomplish the Redemption of man and satisfy the justice of God; then our sway will cease and all our intentions will be frustrated. We have erred in seeking his death. If now we cannot prevent his death, let us see how far his endurance will go and excite his enemies to torture Him with most impious cruelty. Let us stir up their fury against Him; let us suggest to their minds new insults, affronts, ignominies and torments to be inflicted upon his Person; let us drive them to vent upon Him all their wrath in order to exhaust his patience, and let us carefully study the results." These proposals the demons sought to realize, although, on account of the hidden mysteries alluded to above, they found that not all of their plans succeeded. Whenever they incited the executioners to inflict tortures unbecoming his royal and divine Person, the Lord would not permit such indignities farther than was becoming, while He gave free scope to their inhuman barbarities and savage fury in all the rest.

The great Lady of heaven, Mary, likewise interfered in order to curb the insolent malice of Lucifer; for She was well aware of all the designs of the infernal dragon. At times She would make use of her sovereign power as Queen to prevent some of the hellish suggestion to reach the ministers of the Passion; at others She prevented their execution by her prayers, or She enlisted the service of her holy angels to drive away and confuse the persecutors of her Son. Those sufferings, which by her great wisdom She knew, that her Son wished to undergo, She pennitted, fulfilling in all things the divine will. She knew all about the unhappy death of Judas, his torments and place of imprisonment in hell; the bed of ire, which He was to occupy for all eternity, as the master of hypocrisy and the leader of all those who were to deny Christ our Redeemer, as well in thought as in their works, who, according to Jeremias (17,3), leave the veins of living waters, that is Christ, and whose names are written and sealed upon the earth, far from heaven, where are written the names of the predestined. All this the Mother of mercy knew and She wept over his fate most bitterly, praying for the welfare of men and for their salvation from such great blindness and ruinous destruction. Yet in all this She conformed Herself to the just and hidden decrees of divine Providence.

Instruction, which Mary, the Queen of Heaven Gave Me

My daughter, thou art astonished, not without cause, at what thou hast learned and recorded of the unhappy fate of Judas and of the fall of the Apostles, who were all disciples in the school of Christ, nursed at his breast by his doctrine, by the example of his life, and by his miracles, enjoying his sweetest and gentlest intercourse, and many other benefits of my assistance and intercession. But I truly say to thee, if all the children of the Church would attentively consider this example, they would find a salutary exhortation and warning in this mortal state of life against the danger surrounding them even in the midst of the favors and blessings they continually receive at the hands of the Lord. All of them cannot be equal to seeing Him with bodily eyes and having intercourse with Him as the living image of all sanctity. The Apostles received from me personal exhortations and they were eyewitnesses of my blameless and holy conduct; they received great tokens of my kindness and my charity flowed directly from God through me upon them. If they, in the very act of receiving such favors and in the very presence of their God and Savior, forgot all of them and all of their obligation of corresponding to them: who then shall be so presumptuous in this mortal life as not to fear the danger of eternal ruin, no matter how many favors he has received from the Almighty? They were Apostles chosen by their divine Master, their true God; yet one of them fell lower than any other individual of the human race; and the others failed in faith, the foundation of all virtue. Yet all this was conformable to the just judgments of the Most High. Why then should those who are not Apostles, be without fear, who have not so labored in the school of Christ and who have not so merited my intercession?

Concerning the perdition of Judas and of his most just punishment thou hast written enough in order to set forth to what extremes a man can be brought by yielding to vices and to the devil, and by refusing to hear and follow the pleading of grace. I moreover inform thee, that not only the tonnents of the traitorous disciple Judas, but also those of many other Christians, who condemn themselves and shall be sent to the same place of punishment, which was assigned to them and Judas from the beginning of the world, are greater than the torments of many demons. For my most holy Son did not die for the angels, but for men; nor were the fruits and results of the Redemption for the demon, but entirely at the disposal of the children of the Church in the holy Sacraments. The contempt for these incomparable benefits is not properly the sin of the devils, but of the Christians; and therefore they must expect a special and appropriate punishment for this contempt. The mistake of not having recognized Christ as the true God causes the deepest and most tormenting regret to Lucifer and his evil spirits for all eternity. Hence, on account of this error, they are filled with special wrath against those that were redeemed, particularly against the Christians, who derived the greatest benefits from the Redemption and the blood of the Lamb. That is why the devils are so eager to cause forgetfulness and misuse of these graces in them and why afterwards in hell, they are permitted to vent so much the greater fury and wrath upon the wicked Christians. If it were not for the equitable dispositions of divine justice by which the pains are proportioned to the guilt, they would wreck still fiercer vengeance upon them. But the goodness of the Lord extends even to this place and restrains the malice of the demons by his infinite power and wisdom.

In the fall of the other eleven Apostles, I wish, my dearest, that thou learn the frailty of human nature, since even in such great blessings and favors received of the Lord, it easily falls into the habit of gross negligence and ingratitude, such as the Apostles manifested in flying from their heavenly Master and leaving Him in a spirit of doubt. Men incur this danger from their earthly and sensuous inclinations, the result of past sins and of the habits formed by a terrestrial, carnal and sensuous life, void of spirituality. On account of it they desire and love the divine favors and benefits only in a carnal manner. As soon as they fail to find that kind of enjoyment in them, they turn to other sensible enjoyments, are moved by them and lose the true conception of a spiritual life; for they treat it and estimate it according to the low standard of mere sensuality. Hence the Apostles, though they were so greatly favored by my most holy Son, fell into such gross heedlessness and sins; for the miracles, the teachings and the examples affected them only in a sensible manner; and as they, in spite of their being raised to justice and perfection, permitted themselves to be affected by them only outwardly, they were presently disturbed by temptation and yielded to it. They acted like men who had done little to penetrate into the mysteries and into the spirit of what they had seen and heard in the school of their Master. By this example, my daughter, and by my teachings thou oughtest to be well instructed, a spiritual disciple of mine, and not a terrestrial, accustoming thyself to despise mere outwardness, even in favors bestowed upon thee by the Lord or myself. When thou receivest them, do not attach thyself merely to the material or sensible in them, but raise thy mind to the exalted and the spiritual contained therein; to that which is perceived by the interior and spiritual, and not by the animal senses (I Corinthians 2, 14). If even the merely sensible can hinder the spiritual life, how much is this true of that which pertains altogether to earthly, animal and carnal life? Clearly I desire of thee to forget and blot out of thy faculties all images and remembrances of mere creatures in order that thou mayest be lit to receive my salutary teaching and be capable of imitating me.

Jesus Is Taken Prisoner

Jesus the Savior, bound as a prisoner, is dragged to the house of Annas; what happened in connection therewith and what the most Blessed Mother suffered during that time.

Fit were it to speak of the suffering, the affronts and the Death of our Savior Jesus in such vivid and efficacious words, that they enter into the soul like a twoedged sword, piercing with deepest sorrow our inmost hearts (Hebrews 4, 13). Not of an ordinary kind were the pains He suffered and there is no sorrow like unto his sorrow (Lamentations 1, 12). For his body was not like the bodies of the rest of men, nor did the Lord suffer for Himself, nor for his own sins, but for us and for our sins (I Pet. 2, 21). Hence the words and expressions, by which we describe his torments and sorrows, should not be of the common or ordinary kind. But, woe is me, who cannot give sufficient force to my words, and cannot find those my soul seeks in order to manifest this mystery! I will speak according to my capacity and as far as is given me, although my powers constrain and limit the greatness of what I understand. and my inadequate words cannot reach the secret concepts of the heart. Let then the vividness and force of the faith, which we profess as children of the Church, supply what is defective in my words. If our words are but of the ordinary kind, let our compassion and our sorrow be extraordinary; let our thoughts be of the loftiest, our comprehension most real, our consideration of the deepest, our thankfulness heartfelt, and our love most fervent; for all that we can do shall fall short of what the reality demands, of what we owe as servants, as friends, and as children adopted through his most sacred Passion and Death.

Having been taken prisoner and firmly bound, the most meek Lamb Jesus was dragged from the garden to the house of the high priests, first to the house of Annas (John 18, 13). The turbulent band of soldiers and servants, having been advised by the traitorous disciple that his Master was a sorcerer and could easily escape their hands, if they did not carefully bind and chain Him securely before starting on their way, took all precautions inspired by such a mistrust (Mark 14, 44). Lucifer and his compeers of darkness secretly irritated and provoked them to increase their impious and sacrilegious illtreatment of the Lord beyond all bounds of humanity and decency. As they were wining accomplices of Lucifer's malice, they omitted no outrage against the person of their Creator within the limits set them by the

Almighty. They bound Him with a heavy iron chain with such ingenuity, that it encircled as weB the waist as the neck. The two ends of the chain, which remained free, were attached to large rings or handcuffs, with which they manacled the hands of the Lord, who created the heavens, the angels and the whole universe. The hands thus secured and bound, they fastened not in front, but behind. This chain they had brought from the house of Annas the high priest, where it had served to raise the portcullis of a dungeon. They had wrenched it from its place and provided it with padlock handcuffs. But they were not satisfied with this unheardof way of securing a prisoner; for in their distrust they added two pieces of strong rope: the one they wound around the throat of Jesus and, crossing it at the breast, bound it in heavy knots all about the body, leaving two long ends free in front, in order that the servants and soldiers might jerk Him in different directions along the way. The second rope served to tie his arms, being bound likewise around his waist. The two ends of this rope were left hanging free to be used by two other executioners for jerking Him from behind.

In this manner the almighty and holy One permitted Himself to be bound and made helpless, as if He were the most criminal of men and the weakest of the womanborn; for He had taken upon Himself all the iniquities and weaknesses of our sins (Isaias 53, 6). They bound Him in the garden, adding to the chains and ropes insulting blows and vilest language; for like venomous serpents they shot forth their sacrilegious poison in abuse and blasphemy against Him who is adored by angels and men, and who is magnified in heaven and on earth. They left the garden of Olives in great tumult and uproar, guarding the Savior in their midst. Some of them dragged Him along by the ropes in front and others retarded his steps by the ropes hanging from the handcuffs behind. In this manner, with a violence unheard of, they sometimes forced Him to run forward in haste, frequently causing Him to fall; at others they jerked Him backwards; and then again they pulled Him from one side to the other, according to their diabolical whims. Many times they violently threw Him to the ground and as his hands were tied behind He fell upon it with his divine countenance and was severely wounded and lacerated. In his falls they pounced upon Him, inflicting blows and kicks, trampling upon his body and upon his head and face. All these deviltries they accompanied with festive shouts and opprobrious insults, as was foretold by Jeremias (3, 30).

During all this time Lucifer, while inciting these ministers of evil, watched all the actions and movements of our Savior. His patience he thus put to the test in order to find out, whether Jesus was only a man; for this doubt and perplexity tormented his wicked pride above all others. As he was obliged to acknowledge the meekness, patience and sweetness of Christ, his serene majesty without change or disturbance amid all these injuries and sufferings, the infernal dragon was enraged only so much the more and at one time, like one crazed by fury, he attempted to seize the ropes in order that he and his fellowdemons might pull at them more violently than his human foes and thus perhaps overcome the meekness of the Savior. But he was withheld by the most holy Mary, who, from her retreat by a clear vision sawall that happened to her divine Son. When

She noticed this attempt of Lucifer, She made use of her power as sovereign Queen and commanded him to desist. All strength immediately left Lucifer and he could not proceed in his presumptuous intent. It was not becoming that his malice should add to the sufferings and death of the Redeemer in such a manner. He was however given permission to excite all his fellowdemons against the Lord, and these again were left a free hand to incite his mortal enemies among the Jews; since the latter had liberty of will to consent or not. Lucifer used this freedom to its full extent, and therefore said to the other evil spirits: "What kind of a man is this, now born into the world, who by his patience and by his works so torments us and annihilates us? N one ever maintained such equanimity and such longsuffering in tribulations since the time of Adam until now. Never have we found among mortals such humility and meekness. How can we rest, when we see in the world such a rare and powerful example, drawing others after Him? If this is the Messias, He will certainly open heaven and close up the highway, by which we have so far led men into our eternal torments; we shall be vanquished and all our plans will be frustrated. Even if He is but a mere man, I cannot permit such an example for the rest of mankind. Haste then, ministers of my exalted power, let us persecute Him through his human foes, who, obedient to my sway, have conceived of me some of our own furious envy."

The Author of our salvation, hiding his power of annihilating his enemies in order that our Redemption might be the more abundant, submitted to all the consequences of the impious fury which Lucifer and his hellish squadron fomented in the Jews. They dragged Him bound and chained under continued illtreatment to the house of Annas, before whom they presented Him as a malefactor worthy of death. It was the custom of the Jews to present thus bound those criminals who merited capital punishment; and they now made use of this custom in regard to Jesus, in order to intimate his sentence even before the trial. The sacrilegious priest Annas seated himself in proud and arrogant state on the platform or tribunal of a great hall. Immediately Lucifer placed himself at his side with a multitude of evil spirits. The servants and soldiers brought before Him Jesus, bound and fettered, and said: "At last we bring hither this wicked Man, who by his sorceries and evil deeds has disturbed all Jerusalem and Judea. This time his magic art has not availed Him to escape our hands and power."

Our Savior Jesus was attended by innumerable angels, who confessed and adored Him, full of admiration for the incomprehensible judgments of his wisdom (Romans 11, 33) by which the Lord consented to be held as a sinner and a criminal. The iniquitous high priest pretended to be just and zealous for the honor of the Lord, whose life he was seeking. The most meek Lamb was silent and opened not his mouth, as Isaias prophesied (53,7). Imperiously and haughtily the high priest asked Him about his disciples (John 18, 19), and what doctrine He was preaching and teaching. This question was put merely for the purpose of misinterpreting his answer, if Jesus should utter any word that afforded such a chance. But the Master of holiness, who is the Guide and the Corrector of the most wise (Wisdom 7, 15), offered to the eternal Father the humiliation of being presented as a criminal before the high priest and of being questioned by him as a prevaricator and author of a false doctrine. Our Redeemer with an humble and cheerful countenance answered the question as to his doctrines: "I have spoken openly to the world: I have always taught in the synagogue and in the temple, whither all the Jews resort: and in secret I have spoken nothing. Why askest thou Me? ask those, who have heard what I have spoken unto them: behold they know what I have said." As the doctrine of Christ our Lord came from his eternal Father, He spoke for it and defended its honor. He referred them to his hearers, both because those by whom He was now surrounded, would not believe Him and wished to distort all He should say, and because the truth and force of his teachings recommended and forced themselves upon the minds of his greatest enemies by their own excellence.

Concerning the Apostles He said nothing, because it was not necessary on this occasion and because they were not reflecting much credit upon their Master by their present conduct. Though his answer was so full of wisdom and so well suited to the question, yet one of the servants of the highpricst rushed up with raised hand and audaciously struck the venerable and sacred face of Jesus, saying: "Answerest

Thou the high priest so?" The Lord accepted this boundless injury, praying for the one who had inflicted it; and holding Himself ready, if necessary, to turn and offer the other cheek for a second stroke, according to the doctrine He had himself inculcated (Matthew 5, 39). But in order that the atrocious and daring offender might not shamelessly boast of his wickedness, the Lord replied with great tranquillity and meekness: "If I have spoken evil, give testimony of the evil; if well, why strikest thou Me?" O sight most astounding to the supernal spirits! Since this is He, at the mere sound of whose voice the foundations of the heavens tremble and ought to tremble and the whole finnament is shaken! This is the Lord of whom Job says, He is wise of heart and mighty in strength; who hath resisted Him and hath peace? Who hath removed mountains, and they, whom He overthrew in his wrath, knew it not; He who moveth the earth out of its place; who commandeth the sun, and it riseth not; and shutteth up the stars as it were under a seal; who doth things great and incomprehensible, whose wrath no man can resist, and under whom they stoop, that bear up the world (Job 9,4, etc.); this is the One, who for the love of men patiently suffers a servant to strike and wound Him in the face by a buffet!

By the humble and appropriate reply of the Lord, the wickedness of the sacrilegious servant stood reprimanded. Yet neither the shame of this reprimand, nor the shameful negligence of the high priest, which permitted such a criminal unfairness in his very presence, moved either Rim or the other Jews to moderate their conduct toward the Author of life. While this illtreatment of the Lord was going on, saint Peter and the other disciple, who was none other than saint John, arrived at the house of Annas. Saint John, as being well known there, readily obtained entrance, while saint Peter remained outside. Afterwards the servant maid, who was an acquaintance of saint John, allowed also him to enter and see what would happen to the Lord (John 18, 16). The two disciples remained in the portico adjoining the courthall of the priest, and saint Peter approached the fire, which the soldiers, on account of the coldness of the night, had built in the enclosure near the portico. The servant maid, on closer inspection, noticed the depressed bearing of saint Peter. Coming up to him she recognized him as a disciple of Jesus. and said: "Art thou not perhaps one of the disciples of this Man?" This question was asked by the maid with an air of contempt and reproach. Peter in his great weakness and hesitancy yielded to a sense of shame. Overcome also by his fear he answered: "I am not his disciple." Having given this answer, he slipped away to avoid further conversation, and left the premises. But he soon afterwards followed his Master to the house of Caiphas, where he denied Him again at two different times, as I shall relate farther on.

The denial of Peter caused greater pain to the Lord than the buffet which He had received; for this sin was directly opposed and abhorrent to his immense charity, while pains and sufferings were sweet and welcome to Him, since He could thereby atone for our sins. After this first denial of Peter. Christ prayed for him to his eternal Father and ordained that through the intercession of the blessed Mary he should obtain pardon even after the third denial. The great Lady witnessed all that passed from her oratory, as I have said. As She contained in her own breast the propitiatory and sacrifice of her Son and Lord in sacramental form, She directed her petitions and loving aspirations to Him, eliciting most heroic acts of compassion, thanksgiving, adoration and worship. She bitterly wept over the denial of saint Peter, and ceased not, until She perceived that the Lord would not refuse him the necessary helps for effectually rising from his fall. The purest Mother also felt all the wounds and torments of her Son in the same portions of her virginal body as the Savior. When the Lord was bound with the chains and ropes, She felt on her wrists such pains, that the blood oozed from her fingernails, as if they had been really bound and crushed: in the same manner also the other wounds affected her body. As to these tortures were added the sorrows of her heart in seeing Christ our Lord suffer, She shed miraculous tears of blood. She felt also the buffet in the same way, as if that sacrilegious hand had struck at the same time her Son and Herself. At this wicked affront and at the blasphemous insult offered to the Lord, She called out to her holy angels to join Her in magnifying and adoring their Creator in compensation for the injuries offered Him by sinners, and in many most sorrowful lamentations She conferred with the angels concerning the cause of her affliction and mourning.

Instruction, which Mary, the Queen of Heaven Gave Me

My daughter, to great deeds art thou called and invited on account of the divine enlightenment thou receivest concerning the mysteries of the sufferings of my most holy Son and of myself for the human race, and on account of the knowledge which thou hast obtained condeming the small return made by heartless and ungrateful men for all our pains. Thou livest yet in mortal flesh and art thyself subject to this ignorance and weakness; but by the force of truth thou art now roused to great wonder, sorrow and compassion at the want of attention displayed by mortals toward these great sacraments and at the losses sustained by them through their lukewarmness and negligence. What then are the thoughts of the angels and saints, and what are my thoughts in beholding this world and all the faithful in such a dangerous and dreadful state of carelessness, when they have the Passion and Death of my divine Son before their eyes, and when they have me, for their Mother and Intercessor and his most pure life and mine for an example? I tell thee truly, my dearest, only my intercession and the merits of his Son, which I offer to the eternal Father, can delay the punishment and placate his wrath, can retard the destruction of the world and the severe chastisement of the children of the Church, who know his will and fail to fulfill it (John 15, 15). But I am much incensed to find so few who condole with me and try to console my Son in his sorrows, as David says (Psalms 68, 21). This hardness of heart will cause great confusion to them on the day of judgment; since they will then see with irreparable sorrow, not only that they were ungrateful, but inhuman and cruel toward my divine Son, toward me and toward themselves.

Consider then thy duty, my dearest, and raise thyself above all earthly things and above thyself; for I am calling thee and choose thee to imitate and follow me into the solitude, in which I am left by creatures, whom my Son and I have pursued with so many blessings and favors. Weigh in thy heart, how much it cost my Lord to reconcile mankind to the eternal Father (Colos. 1,22) and regain for them his friendship. Weep and afflict thyself that so many should live in such forgetfulness and that so many should labor with all their might at destroying and losing what was bought by the blood of God itsel f and all that I from the first moment of my Conception have sought to procure and am procuring for their salvation. Awaken in thy heart the deepest grief, that in his holy Church there should be many followers of the hypocritical and sacrilegious priests who, under cover of a false piety, still condemn Christ; that pride and sumptuousness with other grave vices should be raised to authority and exalted, while humility, truth, justice and all virtues be so oppressed and debased and avarice and vanity should prevail. Few know the poverty of Christ, and fewer embrace it. Holy faith is hindered and is not spread among the nations on account of the boundless ambition of the mighty of this earth; in many Catholics it is inactive and dead; and whatever should be living, is near to death and to eternal perdition. The counsels of the Gospel are forgotten, its precepts trodden under foot, charity alrpost extinct. My son and true God offers his cheeks in patience and meekness to be buffeted and wounded (Lamentations 3, 30). Who pardons an insult for the sake of imitating Him? Just the contrary is set up as law in this world, not only by the infidels, but by the very children of the faith and of light.

In recognizing these sins I desire that thou imitate me in what I did during the Passion and during my whole life, namely practice the virtues opposed to these vices. As a recompense for their blasphemies, I blessed God; for their oaths, I praised Him; for their unbelief, I excited acts of faith, and so for all the rest of the sins committed. This is what I desire thee to do while living in this world. Fly also the dangerous intercourse with creatures, taught by the example of Peter, for thou art not stronger than he, the Apostle of Christ; and if thou fall in thy weakness, weep over thy fault and immediately seek my intercession. Make up for thy ordinary faults and weaknesses by thy patience in adversities, accept them with a joyous mien and without disturbance, no matter what they may be, whether they be sickness or the molestations coming from creatures, or whether they arise from the opposition of the flesh to the spirit, or from the conflicts with visible or invisible enemies. In all these things canst thou suffer and must thou bear up in faith, hope and magnanimous sentiment. I remind thee, that there is no exercise more profitable and useful for the soul than to suffer: for suffering gives light, undeceives, detaches the heart from visible things and raises it up to the Lord. He will come to meet those in suffering, because He is with the afflicted and sends to them his protection and help (Psalms 40, 15).

Jesus at the House of Caiphas

Christ is dragged to the house of the priest Caiphas, where He is falsely accused and asked whether He is the Son of God; Saint Peter denies him for the second and third time; what most holy Mary did on this occasion, and other mysteries

After Jesus had been thus insulted and struck in the house of Annas, He was sent, bound and fettered as He was, to the priest Caiphas, the father-in-law of Annas, who in that year officiated as the prince and high priest; with him were gathered the scribes and distinguished men of the Jews in order to urge the condemnation of the most innocent Lamb (Matthew 26, 57). The invincible patience and meekness of the Lord of all virtues (Psalms 23, 10) astounded the demons, and they were filled with a confusion and fury so great as no words can describe. Since they could not penetrate into the interior of the sanctuary of his humanity, and since they noticed in the meekest Lord no inordinate movement, nor any sign of complaint, nor any sighing, nor the least attempt at human relief, by which they are wont to search the hearts of other men, the dragon was in the utmost torments and surprised as at something altogether new and unheard of among weak and imperfect mortals. In his fury he redoubled his efforts to irritate the scribes and servants of the priests against Him and excite them to shower their abominable insults and affronts upon his devoted head. In all that the demon suggested to them they showed themselves most eager and they executed it as far as the divine will allowed.

The whole rabble of infernal spirits and merciless foes of Christ left the house of Annas and dragged our Lord Savior through the streets to the house of Caiphas, exercising upon Him all the cruelty of their ignominious fury. The high priests and his attendants broke out in loud derision and laughter, when they saw Jesus brought amid tumultuous noise into their presence and beheld Him now subject to their power and jurisdiction without hope of escape. O mystery of the most exalted wisdom of heaven! O foolishness and ignorance of hell, and blind stupidity of mortals! What a distance immeasurable do I see between the doings of the Most High and yours! At the very time when the King of glory, as the Lord of all virtues and mighty in battles, (Psalms 23, 8), is vanquishing vice, and death, and all sin by the virtues of patience, humility and charity, the world boasts of having overcome and subjected Him to its arrogance and proud presumption! How different were the thoughts of Christ our Lord from those of the ministers of wickedness! The Author of Ii fe offered up to the eternal Father the triumph, which his meekness and humility won over sin; He prayed for the priests, the scribes and servants, presenting his patience and sufferings as a compensation for their persecutions and excusing them on account of their ignorance. The same prayer and petition was sent up at the same time by his blessed Mother, for her enemies and the enemies of her divine Son, thus following and imitating the Lord in all his doings; for, as I have many times said, She sawall as if personally present. Between the actions of the Son and the Mother there was a most sweet and wonderful harmony and a correspondence, most pleasing to the eyes of the eternal Father.

The high priest Caiphas, filled with a deadly envy and hatred against the Master of life, was seated in his chair of state or throne. With him were Lucifer and all his demons, who had come from the house of Annas. The scribes and pharisees, like bloodthirsty wolves, surrounded the gentle Lamb; all of them were full of the exultation of the envious, who see the object of their envy confounded and brought down. By common consent they sought for witnesses, whom they could bribe to bring false testimonies against Jesus our Savior (Matthew 26, 59). Those that had been procured, advanced to proffer their accusations and testimony; but their accusations neither agreed with each other, nor could any of their slander be made to apply to Him, who of his very nature was innocence and holiness (Mark 25, 56; Hebrews 7, 26). In order not to be foiled, they brought two other false witnesses, who deposed, that they had heard Jesus say, He could destroy the temple of God made by the hands of men, and build up another one in three days, not made by them (Mark 16, 58). This testimony did not seem to be of much value, although they founded upon it the accusation, that He arrogated to Himself divine power. Even if this testimony had not been false in itself, the saying, if uttered by the Lord Almighty, would have been infallibly true and could not have been presumptuous or false. But the testimony was false; since the Lord had not uttered these words in reference to the material temple of God, as the witnesses wished to inculcate. At the time when He expelled the buyers and sellers from the temple and when asked by what power He did it, He answered: "Destroy this temple" that is: destroy this sacred humanity, and on the third day I shall restore it, which He certainly did at his Resurrection in testimony of his divine power.

Our Savior Jesus answered not a word to all the calumnies and lies brought forward against his innocence. Caiphas, provoked by the patient silence of the Lord, rose up in his seat and said to Him: "Why dost Thou not answer to what so many witnesses testify against Thee?" But even to this the Lord made no response. For Caiphas and the rest were not only indisposed to believe Him; but they treacherously wished to make use of his answer in order to calumniate Him and satisfy the people in their proceedings against the Galileean, so that they might not be thought to have condemned Him to death without cause. This humble silence, which should have appeased the wicked priest, only infuriated him so much the more because it frustrated his evil purpose. Lucifer, who incited the high priest and all the rest, intently watched the conduct of the Savior. But the intention of the dragon was different from that of the high priest. He merely wanted to irritate the Lord, or to hear some word, by which he could ascertain whether he was true God.

With this purpose satan stirred up Caiphas to the highest pitch of rage and to ask in great wrath and haughtiness: "I adjure Thee by the living God, that Thou tell us, if Thou be the Christ, the Son of God." This question of the high priest certainly convicted him at once of the deepest folly and of dreadful blasphemy; for if it was sincere, he had permitted Christ to be brought before his tribunal in doubt whether He was the true God or not, which would make him guilty of the most formidable and audacious crime. The doubt in such a matter should have been solved in quite another way, conformable to the demands of right reason and justice. Christ our Savior, hearing Himself conjured by the living God, inwardly adored and reverenced the Divinity, though appealed to by such sacrilegious liPsalms Out of reverence for the name of God He therefore answered: "Thou hast said: I am He. Nevertheless I say to you, hereafter you shall see the Son of man (who I am) sitting on the right hand of the power of God, and coming in the clouds of heaven" (Matthew 26, 64). At this divine answer the demons and the men were affected in different ways. Lucifer and his devils could not bear it; but immediately felt a superior force, which hurled them down into the abyss and oppressed them by the truth it contained. And they would not have dared to come again into the presence of Christ our Savior, if the divine Providence had not allowed them to fall again into doubts, whether this Man Christ had really spoken the truth or had merely sought this means of freeing Himself from the hands of the Jews. This uncertainty gave them new courage and they came forth once more to the battlefield. The ultimate triumph over the demons was reserved to the Cross itself, on which the Savior was to vanquish both them and death, as Zachary had prophesied and as will appear later.

But the high priest, furious at the answer of the Lord, instead of looking upon it as a solution of his doubt, rose once more in his seat, and rending his garments as an outward manifestation of his zeal for the honor of God, loudly cried out: "He hath blasphemed; what further need have we of witnesses? Behold, now you have heard the blasphemy: what think you?" (Matthew 26, 65.) The real blasphemy however consisted rather in these words of Caiphas, since he denied the certain fact that Christ was the Son of God by his very nature, and since he attributed to the divine Personality sinfulness, which was directly repugnant to his very nature. Such was the folly of the wicked priest, who by his office should have recognized and proclaimed the universal truth. He made of himself an execrable blasphemer in maintaining that He, who is holiness itself, had blasphemed. Having previously, with satanical instinct, abused his high office in prophesying that the death of one man is better than the ruin of all the people, he now was hindered by his sins from understanding his own prophecy. As the example and the opinions of princes and prelates powerfully stirs up the flattery and subserviency of inferiors, that whole gathering of wickedness was incensed at the Savior Jesus: all exclaimed in a loud voice: "He is guilty of death (Matthew 26, 66), let Him die, let Him die!" Roused by satanic fury they all fell upon their most meek Master and discharged upon Him their wrath. Some of them struck Him in the face, others kicked Him, others tore out his hair, others spat upon his venerable countenance, others slapped or struck Him in the neck, which was a treatment reserved among the Jews only for the most abject and vile of criminals.

Never among men were such outrageous and frightful insults heaped upon anyone as were then heaped upon the Redeemer. Saint Luke and saint Mark say that they covered his face and then struck Him with their hands and fists saying: Prophesy, prophesy to us, Thou Prophet, who was it that struck Thee? The reason for their doing this was mysterious: namely, the joy with which our Savior suffered all these injuries and blasphemies (as I will soon relate) made his face shine forth in extraordinary beauty, and on this account those ministers of wickedness were seized with unbearable consternation and shame. They sought to attribute it to sorcery and magic and, by a resolution befitting also well their unworthiness, they covered the face of the Lord with an unclean cloth, so that they might not be hindered and tormented by its divine light in venting their diabolical wrath. All these affronts, reproaches and insults were seen and felt by the most holy Mary, causing in Her the same pains and wounds in the same parts of her body and at the same time as inflicted upon the Lord. The only difference was, that in our Lord the blows and torments were inflicted by the Jews themselves, while in his most pure Mother they were caused by the Almighty in a miraculous manner and upon request of the Lady. According to natural laws, the vehemence of her interior sorrow and anxiety would have put an end to her life; but She was strengthened by divine power, so as to be able to continue to suffer with her beloved Son and Lord.

The interior acts performed by the Savior under these barbarous and unheard of persecutions, cannot be fathomed by human reason or faculties. Mary alone understood them fully, so as to be able to imitate them with the highest perfection. But as the divine Master now experienced in his own Person, how necessary his sympathy would be for those who were to follow him and practice his doctrine, He exerted Himself so much the more in procuring for them grace and blessings on this occasion, in which He was teaching them by his own example the narrow way of perfection. In the midst of these injuries and torments, and those which followed thereafter, the Lord established for his perfect and chosen souls the beatitudes, which He had promised and proposed to them some time before. He looked upon the poor in spirit, who were to imitate Him in this virtue and said: "Blessed are you in being stripped of the earthly goods; for by my Passion and Death I am to entail upon you the heavenly kingdom as a secure and certain possession of voluntary poverty. Blessed are those who meekly suffer and bear adversities and tribulations; for, besides the joy of having imitated Me, they shall possess the land of the hearts and the good will of men through the peacefulness of their intercourse and the sweetness of their virtues. Blessed are they that weep while they sow in tears; for in them, they shall receive the bread of understanding and life, and they shall afterwards harvest the fruits of everlasting joy and bliss."

"Blessed are also those who hunger and thirst for justice and truth; for I shall earn for them satiation far beyond all their desires, as well in the reign of grace as in the reign of glory. Blessed are they, who, imitating Me in my offers of pardon and friendship, mercifully pity those that offend and persecute them; for I promise them the fulness of mercy from my Father. Blessed be the pure of heart, who imitate Me in crucifying their flesh in order to preserve the purity of their souls. I promise them the "ision of peace and of my Divinity, by becoming like unto Me and by partaking of Me. Blessed are the peaceful, who, yielding their rights, do not resist the evil-minded and deal with them with a sincere and tranquil heart without vengeance; they shall be called my children, because they imitate my eternal Father and I shall write them in my memory and in my mind as my adopted sons. Those that suffer persecution for justice's sake, shall be the blessed heirs of my celestial kingdom, since they suffer with Me; and where lam, there also they shall be in eternity. Rejoice, ye poor; be consoled all ye that are and shall be afflicted; glory in your lot, ye little ones and despised ones of this world, you who suffer in humility and longanimity, suffer with an interior rejoicing; since all of you are following Me in the path of truth. Renounce vanity, despise the pomp and haughtiness of the false and deceitful Babylon; pass ye through the fires and the waters of tribulation until you reach Me, who am the light, the truth and your guide to the eternal rest and refreshment."

In such divine acts and in other aspirations for the good of sinners, our Savior Jesus occupied Himself, while He was surrounded by his malignant enemies as by ravenous dogs (Psalms 21, 17), who pursued Him and satiated Him with insults, affronts, blasphemies and wounds. The Virgin Mary, who was most attentive to all that passed, accompanied Him in all his acts and petitions; for She made the same petitions for his enemies. She took charge of the blessings lavished by her Son upon the just and the predestined, and constituted Herself as their Mother, their Helper and Protectress. In the name of all of them She composed hymns of praise and thanksgiving, because the Lord had assigned such an exalted position in the reign of grace to the despised and poor of this earth. On this account also, and on account of what She afterwards witnessed in the interior of Christ, She chose anew labor and contempt, tribulations and pains as her share during the Passion and during the rest of her most holy life.

Saint Peter had followed the Lord Jesus from the house of Annas to that of Caiphas, although he took care to walk at some distance behind the crowd of enemies for fear that the Jews might seize him. He partly repressed this fear on account of the love of his Master and by the natural courage of his heart. Among the great multitude which crowded in and out of the house of Caiphas and in the darkness, it was not difficult for the Apostle to find entrance into the house of Caiphas. In the gates of the courtyard a servantmaid, who was a portress as in the house of Annas, likewise noticed saint Peter; she immediately went up to the soldiers, who stood at the fire with him and said: "This man is one of those who were wont to accompany Jesus of Nazareth." One of the bystanders said: "Thou art surely a Galilean and one of them." Saint Peter denied it and added an oath, that he was not a disciple of Jesus, immediately leaving the company at the fire. Yet, in his eagerness to see the end, although he left the courtyard, he did not leave the neighborhood. His natural love and compassion for the Lord still caused him to linger in the place, where he saw Him suffer so much. So the Apostle moved about, sometimes nearer, sometimes farther from the hall of justice for nearly an hour. Then a relative of that Malchus, whose ear he had severed. recognized him and said: "Thou art a Galileean and a disciple of Jesus; I saw thee with Him in the garden." Then Peter deeming himself discovered, was seized with still greater fear, and he began to assert with oaths and imprecations, that he knew not the ~1an (Matthew 26, i2). Immediately thereupon the cock crowed the second time, and the prediction of his divine Master, that he should deny Him thrice before the cock crowed twice, was fulfilled to the letter.

The infernal dragon was very anxious to destroy saint Peter. It was Lucifer that incited the two maids, whom he could more easily influence, and afterwards, the soldiers, to molest the Apostle by their attention and inquiries. At the same time as soon as he saw him in his dangerous hesitation and change of mind he tried to disturb saint Peter by vivid imaginations of impending cruelty. Thus tempted, Peter simply denied the Lord at first, added an oath to the second denial, and curses and imprecations against himself at the third. Hence, from one sin he fell into another greater one, yielding to the cruel persecutions of the enemies. But saint Peter, now hearing the crowing of the cock, remembered the warning of his divine Master (Luke 22, 61) ; for, the great Queen in her gentle love having interceded for him, the Lord now cast upon him a look of boundless mercy. From her oratory in the Cenacle She had witnessed the denials together with all the circumstances and the causes which had brought the Apostle to fall so deeply. She had seen him beset with natural fear and much more by the merciless assaults of Lucifer. She threw Herself upon the ground and tearfully interceded for him, alleging his frailty and appealing to the merits of her divine Son. The Lord himself moved the heart of Peter, and by means of the light sent to him, gently reproached him, exhorting him to acknowledge his fault and deplore his sin. Immediately the Apostle left the house of the high priest, bursting with inmost sorrow into bitter tears over his fall. In order to weep in the bitterness of his heart he betook himself to a cave, even now called that of the Crowing Cock; there he poured forth his sorrow and confusion in a flood of tears. At the end of three hours he had obtained pardon for his crimes; and the holy impulses and inspirations had continued during that whole time until he was again restored to grace. The most pure Mother and Queen sent to him one of her angels, who secretly consoled him and excited in him the hope of forgiveness, so that he might not delay his full pardon by want of trust in the goodness of God. The angel was ordered not to manifest himself, because the Apostle had so recently committed his sin. Hence the angel fulfilled his commission without being seen by the Apostle. Saint Peter was consoled and strengthened in his great sorrow by these inspirations and thus obtained full pardon through the intercession of most holy Mary.

Instruction, which Mary, the Queen of Heaven Gave Me

My daughter, the mysterious sacrament of the patience of my Son, by which He bore all the affronts and insults, is a sealed book, which can be opened and understood only by the divine light. Thou hast come to the knowledge of it, as it has been partly laid open for thee, although on account of thy limited powers, thou writest much less than thou hast seen. But as this mystery is being made clear and intelligible to thee in the secret of thy heart, I wish that it be also written there and that thou study by this living example that divine science, which neither flesh nor blood can teach thee. For the world does not know, nor does it merit to know, this science. This philosophy consists in recognizing and loving the happy lot of the poor, the humble, the afflicted, the despised, and those unknown among the children of vanity. This school my most holy and loving Son established in his Church, when He proclaimed and set up the eight beatitudes (Matthew 5,210). Afterwards, when He himself assumed all the sufferings of his Passion, He became for us a Teacher, who practices what He teaches, as thou hast seen. Nevertheless, although this is set before the eyes of the Catholics, and can be plainly read by them in this book of life during their whole earthly pilgrimage, there are but few and scattered souls who enter into this school and study this book, while countless are the wayward and foolish, who ignore this science in their unwillingness to be taught.

All abhor poverty and thirst after riches, none of them being willing to recognize their emptiness. Infinite is the number of those who are carried away by their anger and vengeance, despising meekness. Few deplore their real miseries and struggle merely for terrestrial consolations; scarcely any love justice, or loyally pursue it in their dealings with the neighbors. Mercy is almost extinct, purity of heart is sullied and infringed upon, peace is constrained. None grant pardon, none wish to suffer for justice's sake, yea not even the least of the many torments and pains, which they have so justly merited. Thus, my dearest, there are few who attain the blessings promised by my divine Son and by me. Many times the just indignation and anger of the Almighty is roused against the professors of the true faith; since in the very sight of the living example of their Master, they live almost like infidels; many of them being even more abominable in their lives; for they are properly those who despise the fruits of the Redemption, which they have come to know and confess. In the land of saints they impiously perform the works of wickedness (Isaias 26, 10), and make themselves unworthy of the remedies, which are put at their disposal in more merciful abundance.

Of thee I desire, my daughter, that thou labor valiantly for this blessedness, by seeking to imitate me perfectly according to thy grace of so deeply understanding this doctrine, which is hidden from the prudent and wise of this world (Mark 11, 25). Day for day I manifest to thee new secrets of my wisdom, in order that it may be established in thy heart and thou mayest extend thy hands to valiant deeds (Proverbs 31, 19). And now I will tell thee of an exercise which I practiced and which thou canst imitate to a certain degree. Thou knowest already, that from the very first instant of my Conception I was full of grace, without the least stain or participation of the least effect of original sin. On account of this singular privilege I was blessed in all the virtues, without feeling any repugnance or opposition in the exercise of them, and without being conscious of owing satisfaction for any sins of my own. Nevertheless the divine enlightenment taught me, that I was a Daughter of Adam by nature, which in him had sinned, and therefore I felt bound to humiliate myself to the very dust, even though I shared none of the guilt of that sin. And since I also possessed senses of the same kind as those, through which sin and its effects were contracted and which then and afterwards are operative in present human conditions, I thought myself obliged to mortify them, humiliate them and deprive them of the enjoyment proper to their nature, simply on account of this my parentage from Adam. I acted like a most faithful daughter of a family, who assumes the debt of her father and of her brothers as her own, though she had no share in contracting it, and who strives to pay and satisfy for it the more earnestly, the more she loves her family and the more they are unable to satisfy and free themselves from it, not giving herself any rest until she succeeds. This have I done with all the human race, whose miseries and transgressions I bewailed. Because I was a Daughter of Adam I mortified in me the senses and faculties with which he sinned, and I humiliated myself as one that had fallen and one guilty of his sin and disobedience, though I was entirely free from them. All this I did not only for Adam, but for all who by nature are my breLamentations Thou canst not imitate me under like conditions, since thou art a partaker in his sin and guilt. But I herewith impose upon thee to labor without ceasing for thyself and for thy neighbor, and to humiliate thyself to the very dust; since a contrite and humble heart draws down mercy from the divine goodness.

The Sufferings of Jesus After Peter's Denial

The sufferings of our Savior Jesus Christ after the denial of Peter until morning; and the great sorrw of His holy Mother

The holy Evangelists pass over in silence what and where the Savior suffered after the illtreatment in the house of Caiphas and the denial of saint Peter. But they all take up again the thread of events, when they speak of the council held by them in the morning in order to deliver Him over to Pilate, as will be related in the next chapter. I had some doubts as to the propriety of speaking of this intervening time and of manifesting that which was made known to me concerning it: for it was intimated to me, that all cannot be known in this life, nor is it proper that all should be made known to all men. On the day of judgment these and many other sacraments of the life and the Passion of our Lord shall be published to the whole world. I cannot find words for describing that which I might otherwise manifest: I do not find adequate expressions for my concepts, and much less for the reality itself; all is ineffable and above my capacity. But in order to obey the orders given me, I will say what I am able, so as not to incur the blame of concealing the truth, which directly reproaches and confuses our vanity and forgetfulness. In the presence of heaven I confess my own hardness of heart, in not dying of sorrow and shame for having committed such great sins at such a cost to my God, the Originator of my life and being. We cannot ignore the wickedness and gravity of sin, which caused such ravages in the Author of grace and glory. I would be the most ungrateful of all the womanborn, if I would not now abhor sin more than death and as much as even the demon, and I cannot but intimate and assert, that this is the duty likewise of all the children of the holy Catholic church.

By the ill-treatment, which the Lord received in the presence of Caiphas, the wrath of this high priest and of all his supporters and ministers was much gratified, though not at all satiated. But as it was already past midnight, the whole council of these wicked men resolved to take good care, that the Savior be securely watched and confined until the morning, lest He should escape while they were asleep. For this purpose they ordered Him to be locked, bound as He was, in one of the subterranean dungeons, a prison cell set apart for the most audacious robbers and criminals of the state. Scarcely any light penetrated into this prison to dispel its darkness. It was filled with such uncleanness and stench, that it would have infected the whole house, if it had not been so remote and so well enclosed; for it had not been cleaned for many years, both because it was so deep down and because of the degradation of the criminals that were confined in it; for none thought it worth while making it more habitable than for mere wild beasts, unworthy of all human kindness.

The order of the council of wickedness was executed; the servants dragged the Creator of heaven and earth to that polluted and subterranean dungeon there to imprison Him. As the Lord was still bound with the fetters laid upon Him in the garden, these malicious men freely exercised all the wrathful cruelty with which they were inspired by the prince of darkness; for they dragged Him forward by the ropes, inhumanly causing Him to stumble, and loading Him with kicks and cuffs amid blasphemous imprecations. From the floor in one corner of the subterranean cavern protruded part of a rock or block, which on account of its hardness had not been cut out. To this block, which had the appearance of a piece of column, they now bound and fettered the Lord Jesus with the ends of the ropes, but in a most merciless manner. For they forced Him to approach it and tied Him to it in a stooping position, so that He could neither seat Himself nor stand upright for relief, forcing Him to remain in a most painful and torturing posture. Thus they left Him bound to the rock, closing the prisondoor with a key and giving it in charge of one of the most malicious of their number.

But the infernal dragon rested not in his ancient pride. In the desire of finding out who this Christ was and of overcoming his imperturbable patience. he invented another scheme, to the execution of which he incited the jailer and some others of the servants. He inspired the one who held the key of the divine Treasure Trove, the greatest in heaven and earth, with the idea of inviting some of his equally evilminded companions to descend to the dungeon and entertain themselves for awhile with the Master of life by forcing Him to speak of prophecy, or do some other strange or unheard of thing; for they believed Him to be a diviner or magician. Moved by this diabolical suggestion, he invited some of the soldiers and servants, who readily consented. While they were discussing this matter, a multitude of angels, who assisted the Redeemer in his Passion, when they saw Him so painfully bound in such an improper and polluted place. prostrated themselves before Him, adoring Him as their true God and Master, and showing Him so much the more reverence and worship the more they admired the love which moved Him to subject Himself to such abuse for the sake of mankind. They sang to Him some of the hymns and canticles which his own Mother had composed in his praise, as I have mentioned above. The whole multitude of angelic spirits begged Him, in the name of the same Lady, that, since He would not permit his own almighty power to alleviate the sufferings of his humanity, He give them permission to unfetter and relieve Him of this torturing position and to defend Him from that horde of servants now instigated by the demons to heap upon Him new insults.

The Lord would not permit the angels to render this service and He said to them: "Ministering spirits of my eternal Father, I do not wish to accept any alleviation in my sufferings at present and I desire to undergo these torments and affronts in order to satiate my burning love for men and leave to my chosen friends this example for their imitation and consolation in their sufferings; and in order that all may properly estimate the treasures of grace, which I am gaining for them in great abundance through my pains. At the same time I wish to justify my cause, so that, on the day of my wrath, all may know how justly the reprobate shall be condemned for despising the most bitter sufferings by which I sought to save them. Tell my Mother to console Herself in this tribulation, since the day of rest and gladness shall come. Let Her accompany Me now in my works and sufferings for men; for her affectionate compassion and all her doings, afford Me much pleasure and enjoyment." Thereupon the holy angels betook themselves to their great Queen and Lady and consoled Her with this message, although She already knew in another way the will of her divine Son and all that happened in the house of Caiphas. When She perceived the new cruelty with which they had left Christ the Lord bound in a posture so painful and hard, She felt in her purest body the same pains; just as She had felt that of the blows and cuffs and other insults inflicted upon the Author of life. All the sufferings of the Lord miraculously reacted upon the virginal body of this sincerest Dove; the same pains beset the Son and Mother, and the same sword pierced both their hearts; with only this difference, that Christ suffered as God-man and sole Redeemer of mankind, while Mary suffered as a creature and as a faithful helper of her most holy Son.

When the blessed Queen perceived that this band of vile miscreants, incited by the devil, would be permitted to enter the dungeon, She wept bitterly at what was to happen. Foreseeing the malicious intentions of Lucifer, She held Herself ready to make use of her sovereign power to prevent the executions of any designs upon the person of Christ that would imply indecency, such as the dragon sought to induce those unhappy men to carry out. For although all they did was most unbecoming and irreverent in his regard, yet there were insults, which would have been still more indecent, and by which the demon, not having succeeded hitherto, desired now to try the meek forbearance of the Lord. So exquisite and rare, wonderful and heroic, were the doings of the Lady at this time and during the whole Passion, that they could not worthily be mentioned or becomingly extolled, even if many books were written for this sole object; and as they are indescribable in this life, we must leave their full revelation to the beatific vision.

The ministers of wickedness therefore broke into the dungeon, blasphemously gloating over the expected feast of insult and ridicule, which they were now to hold with the Lord of all creation. Going up to Him they began to defile Him with their loathsome spittle and rain blows and cuffs upon Him with unmentionable and insulting mockery. The Lord opened not his mouth or made any answer; He raised not his divine eyes and lost not the humble serenity of his countenance. The sacrilegious buffoons wished to drive Him to some ridiculous or extraordinary saying or action, so that they might make a laughingstock of Him as a sorcerer; and when they were compelled to witness his unchanging meekness, they allowed themselves to be incited still more by the demons. They untied the divine Master from the stone block and placed Him in the middle of the dungeon, at the same time blindfolding Him with a cloth; there they began to come up one after the other and strike Him with their fists, or slap or kick Him, each one trying to outdo the other in vehemence of their blasphemous cruelty and asking Him to prophesy who had struck Him. This kind of sacrilegious treatment these servants repeated even more often and continued longer than before the tribunal of Annas, to which saint Matthew (26,67), saint Mark (14,65), and saint Luke (22, 64) refer, tacitly including all that followed.

The most meek Lamb silently bore this flood of insults and blasphemies. Lucifer, tormented by his anxious desire of seeing some sign of impatience in Him, was lashed into fury at the equanimity with which the Savior bore it all. Therefore he inspired those slaves and friends of his with the project of despoiling the Lord of all his clothes and pursuing their illtreatment according to suggestions which could only originate in the execrable demon. They readily yielded to this new inspiration and set about its execution. But the most prudent Lady was moved to most tearful prayers and aspiration~ at this abominable attempt and interfered with her power as the Queen. She asked the eternal Father to withdraw his cooperation with the secondary or created causes toward such a beginning and She commanded the faculties of these servants not to perform their natural functions. Thus it happened that none of the ruffians could execute the indecencies, which the demon or their own malice suggested to them. Some of these suggestions they forgot immediately and others they could not follow up, because their limbs became as it were frozen or paralyzed until they again changed their intent. As soon as they desisted the use of their limbs would again be restored, for this was not intended as a punishment, but merely in order to prevent their practicing any indecencies. They were left entirely free to practice those cruelties or indulge in other irreverence, which were not so indecent, or were permitted by the Lord.

The powerful Queen also commanded the demons to be silent and forbade them to follow out the indecent intentions of Lucifer, their leader. By this command of the powerful Lady the dragon completely lost his power in those matters which Mary wished to include in her prohibition. Neither could he further irritate the foolish anger of those depraved men, nor could they go allY further in their indecency than She permitted. But whit:! experiencing within themselves the wonderful and extraordinary effects of her commands, they did not merit to be undeceived or recognize the divine power, although they thus saw themselves alternately paralyzed and suddenly restored to the full use of their powers. They attributed it merely to the sorcery and magic of the Master of truth. In their diabolical infatuation they continued to practice their insulting mockery and tortures upon the person of Christ, until they noticed that the night had already far advanced; then they again tied Him to the column and leaving Him thus bound, they departed with all the demons. It was ordained by the divine Wisdom, that the power of the blessed Mother safeguard propriety and decency due to the person of her most pure Son against the improper intentions of Lucifer and his ministers.

Again the Savior was alone in the dungeon, surrounded by the angelic spirits, who were full of admiration at the doings and the secret judgments of the Lord in what He wished to suffer. They adored Him with deepest reverence and magnified his holy name in exalted praise. The Redeemer of the world addressed a long prayer to his eternal Father for the children of the evangelical Church, for the spreading of the holy faith, and for the Apostles, especially for saint Peter, who during that time was beweeping his sin. He prayed also for those who had injured and tormented Him; above all He included in his prayer his most holy Mother and all those who in imitation of Him were to be afflicted and despised in this world. At the same time He offered up his Passion and his coming Death for these ends. His griefstricken Mother followed Him in these prayers, offering up the same petitions for the children of the Church and for its enemies without any movements of anger, indignation or dislike toward them. Only against the demon was She incensed, because he was entirely incapable of grace on account of his irreparable obstinacy. In sorrowful complaints She addressed the Lord, saying: "Divine Love of my soul, my Son and Lord, Thou art worthy to be reverenced, honored and praised by all creatures, since Thou art the image of the eternal Father and the figure of his substance (Hebrews 1, 3), infinite in thy being and in thy perfections. Thou art the beginning of all holiness (Apocalypse 1,8). But if the creatures are to serve Thee in entire subjection, why do they now, my Lord and God, despise. vilify, insult and torture thy Person, which is worthy of the highest worship and adoration? Why has the malice of men risen to such a pitch? Why has pride dared to raise itself even above heaven? How can envy become so powerful? Thou art the only and unclouded Sun of justice, which enlightens and dispels the darkness of sin (John 1, 9). Thou art the fountain of grace, withholding its waters from no one. Thou art the One, who in his liberal love givest being and life to all that live upon this earth, and all things depend upon Thee, while Thou hast need of none (Acts 17, 28). What then have they seen in thy doings, what have they found in thy Passion, that they should treat Thee in so vile a manner? O most atrocious wickedness of sin, which has so disfigured the heavenly beauty and obscured the light of thy countenance! O cruel sin, which so inhumanly pursues the Repairer of all thy evil consequences! But I understand, my Son and Master, I understand that Thou art the Builder of true love, the Author of human salvation, the Master and Lord of virtues (Psalms 23, 10): Thou wishest to put in practice Thyself what Thou teachest the humble disciples of thy school: Thou wishest to humble pride. confound haughtiness and become the example of eternal salvation to all. And if Thou desirest that all imitate thy ineffable patience and charity, then that is my duty before all others, since I have administered to Thee the material and clothed Thee in this body now subjected to suffering, and wounded, spit upon and buffeted. O would that I alone should suffer these pains, and that Thou. my most innocent Son, be spared! And since this is not possible. let Me suffer with Thee unto death. You, O heavenly spirits. who full of wonder at the longsuffering of my Son recognize his immutable Deity and the innocence and excellence of his humanity, seek ye to compensate for these injuries and blasphemies heaped upon Him by men. Give Him glory and magnificence, wisdom honor, virtue and power (Apocalypse 5, 12). Invite the heavens, the planets and the stars and the elements to acknowledge and confess Him; and see whether there is another sorrow equal to mine!" (Lamentations 1, 12). Such and many more were the sorrowful aspirations of the most pure Lady, in giving vent to the bitterness of her grief and pain.

Peerless was the patience of the heavenly Princess in the Death and Passion of her beloved Son and Lord; so that what She suffered never seemed to Her much, nor her afflictions equal to those demanded by her affection, which was measured only by the love and the dignity of her Son and the greatness of his sufferings. Nor did She in any of the injuries and affronts against the Lord take any account of their being committed against Herself. She reflected not on the share which She herself had in them, although She was made to suffer so much by all of them: She deplored them only in so far as they outraged the divine Personality and caused damage to the aggressors. She prayed for them all, that the Most High might pardon them and grant them salvation from the evils of sin and enlightenment for gaining the fruits of Redemption.

Instruction Given by the Queen of Heaven

My daughter, it is written in the holy Gospels (John 5, 57) that the eternal Father has given to his only Son and mine the power to judge and condemn the reprobate on the last day, the day of universal judgment. This was eminently proper, not only in order that all the sinners may see their Judge, who will sentence them according to the most just will of God; but also in order that they may behold and recognize his humanity, by which they were redeemed, and be confronted in it with the torments and injuries it suffered in order to rescue them from eternal damnation. The same Judge and Lord, who shall judge them, shall also advance the charge. As they carmot answer or satis fy for the crimes with which He charges them, their confusion will be only the beginning of the eternal torments, which they merit by their obstinate ingratitude; for then shall become evident to all the world the greatness of his most merciful and kind Redemption and the justice of their damnation. Great was the sorrow, most bitter the grief, of my most holy Son, that not all should make use of the fruits of his

Redemption. This same thought also pierced my heart and immensely added to the sorrow of seeing Him spit upon, buffeted, and blasphemed more cruelly than can ever be understood by living man. But I understood all these sufferings clearly and as they should be understood; therefore my sorrow was great in proportion to this knowledge, just as it was also the measure of my reverence and love of the person of Christ, my Son and Lord. But next to this sorrow, my greatest one was to know, that after all these death dealing sufferings of the Lord, so many men should still damn themselves even within sight of all the infinite treasures of grace.

I wish that thou imitate and follow me in this sorrow and that thou lament this fearful misfortune; for among all the losses sustained by men, there is none which deserves to be so deplored. nor which can ever be compared to it. My Son and I look with especial love upon those who imitate this sorrow and afflict themselves on account of the perdition of so many souls. Seek thou, my dearest, to distinguish thyself in this exercise and continue to pray: for thou canst scarcely imagine how acceptable are such prayers to the Almighty. But remember his promise, that those who pray shaH receive (Luke 11, 9), and that to those who knock the gates of his infinite treasures shaH be opened. In order that thou mayest have something to offer in return, write into thy heart, what my most holy Son and thy Spouse suffered at the hands of those vile and depraved men, and the invincible patience, meekness and silence with which He submitted to their wicked whims. With this example, labor from now on, that no anger, nor any other passion of a daughter of Adam have any sway over thee. Let an interior and ever active horror of pride, and a dread of injuring thy neighbor, be engendered in thy bosom. Solicitously ask the Lord for patience, meekness, and peacefulness and for a love of suffering and Christ's Cross. Embrace this Cross with a pious affection and follow Christ thy Spouse, in order that thou mayest at last possess Him (Matthew 16, 14).

The Council Convenes on Friday Morning

The Council convenes on Friday morning to substantiate the charges against the Savior Jesus; they send Him to Pilate; most Holy Mary with Saint John and the three Marys go forth to meet Jesus.

At the dawn of Friday morning, say the Evangelists (Matthew 27, 1; Mark 15, 1; Luke 22, 66; John 11, 47), the ancients, the chief priests and scribes, who according to the law were looked upon with greatest respect by the people, gathered together in order to come to a common decision concerning the death of Christ. This they all desired; however they were anxious to preserve the semblance of justice before the people. This council was held in the house of Caiphas, where the Lord was imprisoned. Once more they commanded Him to be brought from the dungeon to the hall of the council in order to be examined. The satellites of justice rushed below to drag Him forth bound and fettered as He was; and while they untied Him from the column of rock, they mocked Him with great contempt saying: "Well now, Jesus of Nazareth, how little have thy miracles helped to defend Thee. The power which Thou didst vaunt, of being able to rebuild the temple in three days, has failed altogether in securing thy escape. But Thou shalt now pay for thy presumption and thy proud aspirations shall be brought low. Come now to the chief priests and to the scribes. They are awaiting Thee to put an end to thy imposition and deliver Thee over to Pilate, who will quickly finish Thee." Having freed the Lord from the rock they dragged Him up to the council. The Lord did not open his lips; but the tortures, the blows and the spittle, with which they had covered Him and which He could not wipe off on account of his bonds, had so disfigured Him, that He now filled the members of the council with a sort of dreadful surprise, but not with compassion. Too great was their envious wrath conceived against the Lord.

They again asked Him to tell them, whether He was the Christ (Luke 22, 1), that is, the Anointed. Just as all their previous questions, so this was put with the malicious determination not to listen or to admit the truth, but to calumniate and fabricate a charge against Him. But the Lord, being perfectly willing to die for the truth, denied it not; at the same time He did not wish to confess it in such a manner that they could despise it, or borrow out of it some color for their calumny; for this was not becoming his innocence and wisdom. Therefore He veiled his answer in such a way, that if the pharisees chose to yield to even the least kindly feeling, they would be able to trace up the mystery hidden in his words; but if they had no such feeling, then should it become clear through their answer, that the evil which they imputed to Him was the result of their wicked intentions and lay not in his answer. He therefore said to them: "If I tell you that I am He of whom you ask, you will not believe what I say; and if I shall ask you, you will not answer, nor release Me. But I tell you, that the Son of man, after this, shall seat Himself at the right hand of the power of God" (Luke 22, 67). The priests answered: "Then thou art the Son of God?" and the Lord replied: "You say that I am." This was as if He had said : You have made a very correct inference, that I am the Son of God; for my works, my doctrines, and your own Scripture, as well as what you are now doing with Me, testify to the fact, that I am the Christ, the One promised in the law.

But this council of the wicked was not disposed to assent to divine truth, although they themselves inferred it very correctly from the antecedents and could easily have believed it. They would neither give assent nor belief, but preferred to call it a blasphemy deserving death. Since the Lord had now reaffirmed what He had said before, they all cried out: "What need have we of further witnesses, since He himself asserts it by his own lips?" And they immediately came to the unanimous conclusion that He should, as one worthy of death, be brought before Pontius Pilate, who governed Judea in the name of the Roman emperor and was the temporal Lord of Palestine. According to the laws of the Roman empire capital punishment was reserved to the senate or the emperor and his representatives in the remote provinces. Cases of such importance as involved the taking away of life were looked upon as worthy of greater attention and as not to be decided without giving the accused a hearing and an opportunity of defense and justification. In these affairs of justice the Roman people yielded to the requirements of natural reason more faithfully than other nations. In regard to this trial of Christ the priests and scribes were pleased with the prospect of having sentence of death passed upon Christ our Lord by the heathen Pilate, because they could then tell the people, that He was condemned by the Roman governor and that this certainly would not have happened if He were not guilty of death. To this extent had they been blinded by their sins and their hypocrisy, that they failed to see how much more guilty and sacrilegious they would even then be than the gentlie judge. But the Lord arranged it thus, in order that by their own behavior before Pilate they might reveal all their wickedness more plainly, as we shall see immediately.

The executioners therefore brought our Savior Jesus Christ to the house of Pilate, in order to present Him, still bound with the same chains and ropes in which they had taken Him from the garden, before his tribunal. The city of Jerusalem was full of strangers, who had come from all Palestine to celebrate the great Pasch of the Lamb and of the unleavened bread. As the rumor of this arrest was already spread among the people, and as the Master of life was known to all of them, a countless multitude gathered in the streets to see Him brought in chains through the streets. They were divided in their opinion concerning the Messiah; some of them shouted out: Let Him die, let Him die, this wicked impostor, who deceives the whole world. Others answered: His doctrines do not appear to be so bad, nor his works; for He has done good to many. Still others, who had believed in Him, were much afflicted and wept; while the whole city was in confusion and uproar concerning the Nazarene. Lucifer and all his demons were very attentive to what was passing; for, seeing himself secretly overcome by the invincible patience and meekness of Christ the Lord, he was stirred to uncontrollable fury by his own pride and haughtiness at the haunting suspicion, that such virtues could not be those of a mere human being. On the other hand, he could not understand how his allowing Himself to be despised and illtreated and his succumbing to so much bodily weakness and, as it were, total annihilation, could ever harmonize with his being true God; for, if He were God, said the dragon to himself, his Divinity would never consent to such annihilation, and the power inherent in his divine nature and communicated to the humanity, would certainly prevent such weakness. Lucifer argued like one who knew nothing of the suspension of the overflow of the divine upon the human nature; which the Lord had secretly ordained for the purpose of securing the highest degree of suffering possible, as I have mentioned above (No. 498). By these misgivings, the pride of satan was lashed to still more furious efforts in the persecution of the Lord so as to ascertain who this One was that knew how to suffer torments in such a manner.

The sun had already arisen while these things happened and the most holy Mother, who saw it all from afar, now resolved to leave her retreat and follow her divine Son to the house of Pilate and to his death on the Cross. When the great Queen and Lady was about to set forth from the Cenacle, saint John arrived, in order to give an account of all that was happening; for the beloved disciple at that time did not know of the visions, by which all the doings and sufferings of her most holy Son were manifest to the blessed Mother. After the denial of saint

Peter, saint John had retired and had observed, more from afar what was going on. Recognizing also the wickedness of his flight in the garden, he confessed it to the Mother of God and asked her pardon as soon as he came into her presence; and then he gave an account of all that passed in his heart and of what he had done and what he had seen in following his Master. Saint John thought it well to prepare the afflicted Mother for her meeting with her most holy Son, in order that She might not be overcome by the fearful spectacle of his present condition. Therefore He sought to impress Her beforehand with some image of his sufferings by saying: "O my Lady, in what a state of suffering is our divine Master! The sight of Him cannot but break one's heart; for by the buffets and the blows and by the spittle, his most beautiful countenance is so disfigured and defiled, that Thou wilt scarcely recognize Him with thy own eyes." The most prudent Lady listened to his description, as if She knew nothing of the events; but She broke out in bitterest tears of heartrending sorrow. The holy women, who had came forth with the Lady, also listened to saint John, and all of them were filled with grief and terror at his words. The Queen of heaven asked the Apostle to accompany Her and the devout women, and, exhorting them all, She said: "Let us hasten our steps, in order that my eyes may see the Son of the eternal Father, who took human form in my womb; and you shall see, my dearest friends, to what the love of mankind has driven Him, my Lord and God, and what it costs Him to redeem men from sin and death, and to open for them the gates of heaven."

The Queen of heaven set forth through the streets of Jerusalem accompanied by saint John and by some holy women. Of these not all, but only the three Marys and other very pious women, followed Her to the end. With Her were also the angels of her guard, whom She asked to open a way for Her to her divine Son. The holy angels obeyed and acted as her guard. On the streets She heard the people expressing their i various opinions and sentiments concerning the sorrow, ful events now transpiring in reference to Jesus of Nazareth. The more kindly hearted lamented over his fate. I and they were fewest in number. Others spake about the intention of his enemies to cruci fy Him; others related where He now was and how He was conducted : through the streets, bound as a criminal; others spoke of : the illtreatment He was undergoing; others asked, what evil He had done, that He should be so misused; others again in their astonishment and in their doubts, exclaimed: To this then have his miracles brought Him! Without a doubt they were all impostures, since He cannot defend or free

Himself! All the streets and squares were full of people and excited talk. But in the midst of this excitement the invincible Queen, though filled with the bitterest sorrow, preserved her constancy and composure, praying for the unbelievers and the evildoers, as if She had no other care than to implore grace and pardon for their sins. She loved them as sincerely as if She were receiving favors and blessings at their hands. She permitted no indignation or anger to arise in her heart against the sacrilegious ministers of the Passion and Death of her beloved Son, nor any sign of such feelings in her exterior conduct. All of them She looked upon with charity and the desire of doing them good.

592. Some of them that met Her on the streets, recognized Her as the Mother of Jesus of Nazareth and moved by their natural compassion, said: "O sorrowful Mother! What a misfortune has overtaken Thee! How must thy heart be wounded and lacerated with grief!" Others again impiously said: "Why didst Thou permit Him to introduce such novelties among the people? It would have been better to restrain and dissuade Him; but it will be a warning for other mothers, and they will learn from thy misfortunes, how to instruct their children." These and other more horrible sentiments were expressed in the hearing of this sincerest Dove; but all of them She met with burning charity, accepting the pity of the kindhearted, and suffering the malice of the unbelievers. She was not surprised at the ingratitude of the unresponsive and the ignorant; but implored the eternal Father to impart suitable blessings to all.

Through the swarming and confused crowds the angels conducted the Empress of heaven to a sharp turn of the street, where She met her most holy Son. With the profoundest reverence She prostrated Herself before his sovereign Person and adored it more fervently and with a reverence more deep and more ardent than ever was given or ever shall be given to it by an the creatures. She arose and then the Mother and Son looked upon each other with ineffable tenderness, interiorly conversing with each other in transports of an unspeakable sorrow. The most prudent Lady stepped aside and then followed Christ our Lord, continuing at a distance her interior communication with Him and with the eternal Father. The words of her soul are not for the mortal and corruptible tongue: but among other prayers the afflicted Mother said: "Most high God and my Son, I am aware of thy burning love for men, which leads Thee to hide the infinite power of thy Divinity beneath a form of passible flesh (Philippians 2, 7) formed in my womb. I confess thy incomprehensible wisdom in accepting such affronts and torments, and in sacrificing Thyself, who art the Lord of all creation, for the rescue of man, who is but a servant, dust and ashes (Genesis 3, 19). Thy goodness is to be praised, blessed, confessed and magnified by an creatures; but how shall I, thy Mother, ever cease to desire that all these injuries be heaped upon me and not upon thy divine Person, who art the beauty of the angels and the glory of the eternal Father? How shall I cease to desire the end of these pains? With what sorrow is my heart filled to behold Thee so afflicted, thy most beautiful countenance so defiled, and when I see, that to the Creator and Redeemer alone is denied pity and compassion in such bitter suffering? But if it is not possible, that I relieve Thee as Mother, do Thou accept my sorrowful sacrifice in not being able to bring Thee the relief which is due to the true and holy Son of God."

The image of her divine Son, thus wounded, defiled and bound, remained so firmly fixed and imprinted in the soul of our Queen, that during her life it was never effaced, and remained in her mind as distinctly, as if She were continually beholding Him with her own eyes. Christ our God arrived at the house of Pilate, followed by many of the council and a countless multitude of the people. The Jews, wishing to preserve themselves as clean before the law as possible for the celebration of the Pasch and the unleavened bread, excused themselves before Pilate for their refusing to enter the pretorium or court of Pilate in presenting Jesus. As most absurd hypocrites they paid no attention to the sacrilegious uncleanness, with which their souls were affected in becoming the murderers of the innocent God-man. Pilate, although a heathen, yielded to their ceremonious scruples, and seeing that they hesitated to enter his pretorium, he went out to meet them. According to the formality customary among the Romans, he asked them (John 18, 28) : "What accusation have you against this Man?" They answered: "Jf He were not a criminal, we would not have brought Him to thee thus bound and fettered." This was as much as to say: We have convinced ourselves of his misdeeds and we are so attached to justice and to our obligations, that we would not have begun any proceedings against Him, if He were not a great malefactor. But Pilate pressed his inquiry and said: "What then are the misdeeds, of which He has made Himself guilty?" They answered: "He is convicted of disturbing the commonwealth, He wishes to make Himself our king and forbids paying tribute to Caesar (Luke 23, 2); He claims to be the son of God. and has preached a new doctrine, commencing in Galilee, through all Judea and Jerusalem." "Take Him then yourselves," said Pilate, "and judge Him according to your laws; I do not find a just cause for proceeding against Him." But the Jews replied: "It is not permitted us to sentence anyone to death, nor to execute such a sentence."

The most holy Mary, with saint John and the women who followed Her, was present at this interview; for the holy angels made room for them where they could hear and see all that was passing. Shielded by her mantle She wept tears of blood, pressed forth by the sorrow which pierced her virginal heart. In her interior acts of virtue She faithfully reproduced those practiced by her most holy Son, while in her pains and endurance She copied those of his body. She asked the eternal Father to grant Her the favor of not losing sight of her divine Son, as far as was naturally possible, until his Death; and this was conceded to Her, excepting during the time in which He was in prison. Considering it but just, that amid all the false accusations of the Jews the innocence of the Savior and the injustice of the sentence should become known, the most prudent Lady fervently prayed, that the judge be not deceived and that he obtain clearest insight into Christ's being delivered over to him by the envy of the priests and scribes. In virtue of this prayer, Pilate clearly saw the truth, was convinced of the innocence of Christ and of his being a victim of their envy (Matthew 28, 18). On her account also the Lord declared Himself more openly to Pilate, although the latter did not cooperate with the truth made known to him. It profited not him, but us; and it served to convict the priests and pharisees of their treachery.

In their wrath the Jews are anxious to dispose Pilate favorably toward their project and they wished him to pronounce the sentence of death against Jesus without the least delay. When they perceived his hesitation, they ferociously raised their voices, accusing Jesus over and over again of revolting against the government of Judea, deceiving and stirring up the people (Luke 23, 5), calling Himself Christ, that is an anointed King. This malicious accusation they pressed particularly, hoping to stir Pilate to fear for the temporal welfare of his government, with which he was charged by the Romans. Among the Jews the kings were anointed; therefore they insisted, that Jesus in having called Himself Christ, intended to constitute Himself as King, and, as Pilate was a heathen and knew nothing of the anointing of kings, they wished to persuade him, that calling oneself Christ among the Jews was identical with calling oneself king of the Jews. Pilate asked the Lord: "What dost Thou answer to the accusations which they bring against Thee?" But the Savior answered not one word in the presence of his accusers, causing much wonder in Pilate at such silence and patience. But, desiring to inquire more closely, whether Jesus was truly a King, he withdrew from the clamoring Jews and brought Jesus into the pretorium. There he asked Him face to face: "Tell me, can it be that Thou art a King of the Jews?" Pilate could not bring himself to think that He was a King in fact; since he knew that Christ was not reigning. Therefore he wished to find out, whether Jesus claimed or really possessed any right to the title of King. Our Savior answered him: "Sayest thou this thing of thyself, or have others told it thee of Me?" (John 18,34). Pilate replied: "Am I a Jew? Thy own nation and the chief priests have delivered Thee up to me. "That hast Thou done?" Jesus answered: "My kingdom is not of this world. If my kingdom were of this world, my servants would certainly strive that I be not delivered to the Jews: but now my kingdom is not from hence." The judge partly believed this assertion of Jesus and therefore answered: "Art Thou a king then?" Jesus answered: "Thou sayest that I am a king. For this I was born and for this I came into the world. Every one that is of the Truth, heareth my voice." Pilate wondered at this answer and asked: "What is truth?" But without waiting for an answer, he left Him in the pretorium, and said to the Jews: "I find no cause in Him. But you have a custom, that I should release one unto you at the Pasch: will you, therefore, that I release unto you the King of the Jews, or Barabbas?" This Barabbas was a thief and murderer, who had killed some one in a quarrel. All the people raised their voice and said: "We desire that you release Barabbas, and crucify Jesus." In this demand they persisted until it was granted.

Pilate was much disturbed by the answers of Jesus and the obstinacy of the Jews. For on the one hand, seeing that they were so determined on the death of Jesus, he well knew, that it would be difficult to satisfy them without consenting to their demands; and on the other hand, he clearly saw that they persecuted Him out of mortal envy and that their accusations about his disturbing the people, were false and ridiculous (Matthew 17, 18). In regard to the imputation, that He had made Himself King, he was likewise satisfied of the contrary by the answers of Christ and by his humility, poverty and patient forbearance toward their calumnies. By the light and grace which Pilate received, he became fully convinced that Jesus was truly innocent, although he never pierced the mystery of his Divinity and the greatness of this innocence. The living words of Christ created an exalted idea of Him in his mind and made him think that some great mystery was connected with Him; therefore he desired to free Him and finally determined to send Him to Herod. But all these shifts failed, because Pilate made himself unworthy by his sin and paid attention only to his worldly ,prospects, allowing himself to be governed by them and not by the dictates of justice, but more by the suggestions of Lucifer, as I have related above, than by the truth, which he so clearly knew. Fully understanding the true circumstances, he acted the part of a wicked judge in continuing to treat the cause of an innocent Man with those who were his declared enemies and false accusers. Thus he committed the still greater crime of condemning Jesus to such an inhuman scourging and then to death, without having any other cause than to satisfy the Jews.

But though Pilate for these and other reasons was a most wicked and unjust judge in thus condemning Christ, whom he held to be a mere man, though good and innocent; yet his crime was much smaller than that of the priests and pharisees. And this not only because they were moved by envy, cruelty and other vices, but also because they sinned in not acknowledging Christ as their true Messias and Redeemer, God and Man, such as He had been promised in the Law, which they believed and professed. For their own condemnation the Lord permitted, that in their very accusations they called Him Christ and anointed King, thus confessing with their lips what they denied and discredited in their proceedings. They were bound to believe this truth, which they confessed in their words, and thus come to the understanding of the true anointment of the Savior, which was an unction prefigured in the kings and priests of the olden times and consisted in the anointment mentioned by David (Psalms 44, 8) and different from theirs; namely, the unction of the Divinity resulting from its union with the humanity and by which Christ's soul was anointed with the gifts of grace and glory corresponding to the hypostatic union. All these mysteries of truth were providentially hidden beneath the accusations of the Jews, although they in their perfidy would not believe them, and in their envy interpreted them falsely. For they imputed to the Savior the desire of making Himself king, without his being one, while just the contrary was really the truth: He was in every respect the supreme Lord, but did not wish to show or make use of the power of a temporal king. He had not come into this world to command men, but to obey (Matthew 20, 28). Still greater was the blindness of the Jews in hoping for a temporal king as their Messias and at the same time calumniously asserting that Jesus made of Himself a king. It seems that they sought for their Messias a King so powerful, that they would not be able to resist Him; although they then would have to receive a king by compulsion and not with the free will benevolently desired by the Lord.

Our great Lady profoundly understood these hidden sacraments and the wisdom of her chaste heart made use of them to excite heroic acts of all the virtues. Other children of Adam, conceived in original sin and defiled by their own, are wont to be disturbed and oppressed in proportion to the increase of sorrow and tribulation, and excited to impatience and other inordinate passions; but most holy Mary, who was actuated not by sin or its effects, or by mere nature, was impelled by exalted grace to just the contrary course of action.

For the great persecutions and the vast waters of affliction and sorrow extinguished not in her bosom the fire of divine love (Canticles 8, 7); but they were new incentives to the fires of divine love in her soul, breaking forth in petitions for the sinners so much the more ardently, as the malice of men reached greater excesses. O Queen of virtues, Mistress of creatures and sweetest Mother of mercy! How hard of heart am I, how slow and insensible, that my soul is not annihilated by sorrow at what I understand of thy sufferings and those of thy divine Son! That I still live, knowing all I do know, should cause in me a sorrow unto death. It is a crime against love and piety to beg favors from the innocent, whom we see suffering torments. With what truth can we then say as creatures, that we love God, our Redeemer, and Thee, my Queen, who art his Mother, if Thou and He alone drink out the chalice of such torments and pains, while we are draining the chalice of the pleasures of Babylon? O that I might understand this truth! O that it might penetrate into my deepest heart and that it might pierce my very soul at the sight of such inhuman torments of my Savior and his afflicted Mother! How can I conceive, that anyone can do me an injustice in persecuting me, that they offend me by despising me, that they insult me by abhorring me? How can I complain of suffering, even if I am blamed, neglected and contemned by the world? O great Chieftainess of the martyrs, Queen of the courageous, Mistress of all the imitators of thy Son, if I am thy daughter and disciple, as Thou condescendest to call me, and as my Lord wishes me to merit, do not reject my longing desire to follow thy footsteps on the way of the cross. If in my weakness I have fallen. do Thou, my Lady and Mother, obtain for me the courage of a contrite heart, justly humiliated on account of its vile ingratitude. Gain for me through thy prayers the love of the eternal Father, which is so precious, that only thy powerful intercession can obtain it and only my Lord and Redeemer can merit it for me.

Instruction, which Mary, the Queen of Heaven Gave Me

My daughter, great is the neglect and the inattention of men in failing to consider the works of my most holy Son and to penetrate with humble reverence the mysteries which He has concealed within them for the salvation of all. But many do not know, and others are astonished, that the Lord should have consented to be presented as a criminal before iniquitous judges and be examined by them as a wicked malefactor; that they should have been allowed to treat Him as an ignorant fool; and that He should not have made use of his divine wisdom to defend his innocence, convict the Jews and all his enemies of their malice, since He could so easily have done it. But these sentiments of wonder should be especially united to a deep veneration for the judgments of the Lord, who disposed all things connected with the Redemption according to his equity, goodness and rectitude and in a manner befitting all his attributes, denying none of his enemies sufficient help to follow the good, if only they wished to use their freedom for that purpose. He wished all of them to be saved (I Timothy 2,4), and if not all of them attained this salvation, no one can justly complain of his superabundant kindness.

But besides this, I wish, my dearest, that thou understand the instructive lessons contained in these works; for in each one of them my Son acted as Redeemer and Teacher of men. In the silence and the meekness, which He maintained during his Passion, permitting Himself to be reputed as a wicket!. and foolish man, He left to mankind a lesson just as important as it is unnoticed and unpracticed by the children of Adam. Because they do not heed the contagion of Lucifer through sin, which is perpetuated in the world, they do not seek in the Physician the medicine of suffering, which the Lord in his immense charity has left to the world in word and deed. Let men then consider themselves conceived in sin (Psalms 5-, 7), and let them realize how strong has grown in them the hellish seed of pride, of presumption, vanity, self esteem, avarice, hypocrisy, deceitfulness, and all other vices. Each one ordinarily seeks to advance his honor and vainglory, struggling to be applauded and renowned. The learned and those who think themselves wise, wish to be applauded and looked up to, bragging about their knowledge. The unlearned try to appear wise. The rich glory in their riches and wish to be respected on their account. The poor strive to be and appear rich, anxious to gain the approbation of the wealthy. The powerful seek to be feared, worshipped and obeyed. All of them are pursuing the same deceit of seeking to appear what they are not in fact, and fail in reality to come up to what they appear to be. They palliate their faults, extol their virtues and abilities, they attribute to themselves the goods and the blessings as if they had not received them from God. They receive them as if they were their due and not owing to his liberal kindness; instead of being thankful for them they abuse them as weapons against God and against their own selves. Commonly all are swollen up by the mortal poison of the serpent and so much the more anxious to drink it, the more deeply they are already wounded and weakened by his lamentable assaults. The way of the cross and imitation of Christ in humble Christian sincerity is deserted, because they are so few that walk upon it.

In order to crush the head of Lucifer and overcome pride and arrogance, my Son observed this patient silence in his Passion, pennitting Himself to be treated as an ignorant and foolish criminal. As the Teacher of this philosophy and as the Physician of the sickness of sin, He would not deny the charges nor defend or justify Himself, nor refute those who accused Him, showing us by his own living example, how to oppose and counteract the intentions of the serpent. In the Lord was that teaching of the wise man put into practice: More precious is a little foolishness in its time than wisdom and glory (Ecclesiastes 10, 1); for it is better that human frailty be at times considered ignorant and wicked, than that it make a vain show of virtue and wisdom. Infinite is the number of those who are entangled in this dangerous error, who, desiring to appear wise, speak much and multiply words like the foolish (Ecclesiastes I, 14). They only lose what they strive so much to attain, since they become known as foolish. All these vices arise from the pride rooted in human nature. But do thou, my daughter, preserve the doctrine of my divine Son and that which comes from me. Abhor human ostentation, suffer in silence and let the world consider thee ignorant; for it does not know where true wisdom dwells.

Pilate Sends the Jews With Jesus to Herod

Pilate sends the Jews with Jesus and their accusations to Herod, where they advance their charges; Herod treats Jesus with contempt and sends Him back to Pilate; Mary follows the Savior; other happenings in connection.

One of the accusations of the Jews and the priests before Pilate was, that Jesus our Savior had begun to stir up the people by his preaching in the province of Galilee (Luke 23, 6). This caused Pilate to inquire, whether He was a Galilean; and as they told him, that Jesus was born and raised in that country, he thought this circumstance useful for the solution of his difficulties in regard to Jesus and for escaping the molestations of the Jews, who so urgently demanded his death. Herod was at that time in Jerusalem, celebrating the Pasch of the Jews. He was the son of the first Herod, who had murdered the Innocents to procure the death of Jesus soon after his birth (Matthew 2, 16). This murderer had become a proselyte of the Jews at the time of his marriage with a Jewish woman. On this account his son Herod likewise observed the law of Moses, and he had come to Jerusalem from Galilee, of which he was governor. Pilate was at enmity with Herod, for the two governed the two principal provinces of Palestine, namely, Judea and Galilee, and a short time before it had happened that Pilate, in his zeal for the supremacy of the Roman empire, had murdered some Galileeans during a public function in the temple, mixing the blood of the insurgents with that of the holy sacrifices. Herod was highly incensed at this sacrilege, and Pilate, in order to afford him some satisfaction without much trouble to himself, resolved to send to him Christ the Lord to be examined and judged as one of the subjects of Herod's sway. Pilate also expected that Herod would set Jesus free as being innocent and a Victim of the malice and envy of the priests and scribes.

Christ our Lord therefore went forth from the house of Pilate to the palace of Herod, being still bound and chained as before and accompanied by the scribes and priests as his accusers. There were also a large number of soldiers and servants, who dragged Him along by the ropes and cleared the streets, which had been filled with multitudes of the people to see the spectacle. The military broke their way through the crowds; and as the servants and priests were thirsting so eagerly for the blood of the Savior and wished to shed it on this very day, they hastened with the Lord through the streets nearly on a run and with great tumult. Mary also set forth from the house of Pilate with her company in order to follow her sweetest Son Jesus and accompany Him on the ways, which He was still to go until his death on the Cross. It would not have been possible for the Lady to follow her Beloved closely enough to be in his sight, if She had not ordered her holy angels to open a way for Her. They made it possible for Her to be constantly near her Son, so that She could enjoy his presence, though that also brought with it only a fuller participation in all torments and sorrows. She obtained the fulfillment of all her wishes; for walking along through the streets near the Savior She saw and heard the insults of the servants, the blows they dealt Him, the reproaches of the people, expressed either as their own or repeated from hearsay.

When Herod was informed that Pilate would send Jesus of Nazareth to him, he was highly pleased. He knew that Jesus was a great friend of John the Baptist, whom he had ordered to be put to death (Mark 6, 27), and had heard many reports of his preaching. In vain and foolish curiosity he harbored the desire of seeing Jesus do something new and extraordinary for his entertainment and wonder (Luke 23, 8). The Author of life therefore came into the presence of the murderer Herod, against whom the blood of the Baptist was calling more loudly to this same Lord for vengeance, than in its time the blood of Abel (Genesis 4, 10). nut the unhappy adulterer, ignorant of the terrible judgment c;>f the Almighty, received Him with loud laughter as an enchanter and conjurer. In this dreadful misconception he commenced to examine and question Him, persuaded that he could thereby induce Him to work some miracle to satisfy his curiosity. But the Master of wisdom and prudence, standing with an humble reserve before his most unworthy judge, answered him not a word. For on account of his evildoing he well merited the punishment of not hearing the words of life, which he would certainly have heard if he had been disposed to listen to them with reverence.

The princes and priests of the Jews stood around. continually rehearsing the same accusations and charges which they had advanced in the presence of Pilate. But the Lord maintained silence also in regard to these calumnies, much to the disappointment of Herod. In his presence the Lord would not open his lips, neither in order to answer his questions, nor in order to refute the accusations. Herod was altogether unworthy of hearing the truth, this being his greatest punishment and the punishment most to be dreaded by all the princes and the powerful of this earth. Herod was much put out by the silence and meekness of our Savior and was much disappointed in his vain curiosity. But the unjust judge tried to hide his confusion by mocking and ridiculing the innocent Master with his whole cohort of soldiers and ordering him to be sent back to Pilate. Having made fun of the reserve of the Lord, the servants of Herod joined in treating Him as a fool and as one deficient in mind and they clothed Him in a white garment, in order to mark Him as insane and to be avoided as dangerous. But by the hidden providence of the Most High this dress signified the purity and innocence of the Savior, and these ministers of wickedness were thus unwittingly giving testimony of the truth, which they were trying to obscure in deriding the miraculous power of the Lord.

Herod showed himself thankful to Pilate for the courtesy of sending Jesus of Nazareth to be judged before his tribunal. He informed Pilate, that he found no cause in Him, but held Him to be an ignorant man of no consequence whatever. By the secret judgments of divine Wisdom, Herod and Pilate were reconciled on that day and thenceforward remained friends. Conducted by many soldiers, both of Herod and Pilate, amid a still greater concourse, tumult, and excitement of the people, Jesus returned from Herod to Pilate. For the very ones who had some time before hailed and venerated Him as the Savior and Messias, blessed of the Lord (Matthew 21, 9), now perverted by the priests and magistrates, had changed their minds, and they despised and condemned the same Lord, whom they had so shortly before reverenced and glorified. For of such influence is usually the erroneous example of the chiefs in misleading the people. In the midst of all this confusion and ignominy the Lord passed along, repeating within Himself in unspeakable love, humility and patience, those words, which He had long before spoken by the mouth of David: "I am a wonn and no man; the reproach of men and the outcast of people. All they that saw me have laughed me to scorn: they have spoken with their lips and wagged the head" (Psalms 21, 7). The Lord was a worm and no man, not only because He was not engendered like the rest of men, and because He was not merely and solely a man, being true God and man; but also because He was not treated like a man, but like a wretched and despised worm. Amid all the scorn with which He was overwhelmed and trodden under foot, He made no more outcry than an humble worm-let, which is despised and crushed as a most vile and despicable creature. All the innumerable multitudes that saw our Redeemer spoke of Him with wagging heads, as if retracting their previous conception and opinion of this Prophet of Nazareth.

Although his afflicted Mother was made interiorly aware of all that happened, She was not present in body when the priests advanced their insulting accusations before Herod, and when he sputtered forth his questions to the Author of life. She remained outside of the hall of judgment, whither they had taken the Lord. But when He came forth from the hall She met him and They looked upon each other in reciprocal sorrow of their souls, such as corresponded to the love between such a Son and Mother. The sight of the white vestment, by which they proclaimed Him fit to be treated only as an insane fool, pierced her heart with new sorrow; though She alone, of all mankind, recognized the mystery of his purity and innocence indicated by this vestment. She adored Him in it with deepest reverence and followed Him through the streets back to the house of Pilate; for in this house was to be executed the divine decree for our salvation. On this way from Herod to Pilate it happened, that on account of the crush of the people and on account of the haste, they tripped Him up and threw Him on the ground several times. By their cruel pulling at the ropes witl1 which He was bound, they caused the blood to flow from his sacred veins. His hands being tied, He could not easily help Himself to rise from his falls. Therefore the multitudes of the people, who followed and who were neither able, nor cared to stop in their onward rush, stepped upon the divine Lord, treading Him under foot and kicking Him. The blows and wounds He thus received, instead of stirring the compassion of the soldiers, only excited them to loud laughter; for, instigated by the demons, they had become devQid of all human compassion, no less than so many wild beasts.

At the sight of such unmeasured cruelty, the most Eorrowful and loving Mother was moved to deepest compassion, and turning to her holy angels She commanded them to gather up the divine blood in order that it might not be trodden upon and dishonored by the feet of sinners. This the heavenly servants willingly fulfilled. She commanded also, that if her divine Son should again fall to the earth, they hasten to his assistance and prevent these evildoers from injuring and stepping on his most sacred body. But She was the most prudent of all mortals, She did not wish them to execute her command, unless it met the approval of the Lord; and therefore She urged them to make this proposal themselves and ask his permission, representing to Him at the same time her anguish as his Mother in seeing Him thus irreverently SUbjected to the feet of sinners. In order to so much the sooner move the Lord to grant this petition, She begged Him through: the holy angels, that He commute this humiliation of being trodden upon and

81

crushed by the rabble into an act of obedience in complying with the petition of his afflicted Mother, who at the same time acknowledged Herself as his slave and formed of the dust. All these petitions of his blessed Mother the angels presented to the Lord Christ in her name; not that He was ignorant of them. since He knew all things and was Himself the instigator of them through his divine grace, but the Lord desires in all these matters a regard for the due process of reason. The great Lady was aware of this desire and in her most exalted wisdom practiced virtues in diverse ways and by diverse acti~ities, unimpeded by the foreknowledge of the Lord concerning all things.

Our Savior Jesus yielded to the desire and petitions of his most blessed Mother and gave the angels permission to execute her requests as her ministers. During the rest of the passage to the house of Pilate they would not permit the Lord to be tripped or cast to the ground, or to be stepped upon by the crowd as had happened before. But in regard to other injuries, He allowed the stupid wrath and blind malice of the servants of the law and of the populace to vent themselves freely and fully upon his divine Person. His most holy Mother heard and saw all with an unconquered but lacerated heart. In a proportionate manner this was also witnessed by the other Marys and saint John, who with ceaseless tears followed the Lord in company with his purest Mother. I do not stop to describe the sorrows of these and other pious women, who attended upon the Queen, because I would go too wide of my subject, especially if I were to describe the doings of Magdalen, most distinguished in her ardent love of Christ and most pleasing to the Savior. For to her we must apply, what Christ himself said when He justified Her: that those love most to whom the greater sins are forgiven (Luke 7, 43).

Pilate was again confronted with Jesus in his palace and was bestormed anew by the Jews to condemn Him to death of the cross. Convinced of the innocence of Christ and of the mortal envy of the Jews, he was much put out at Herod's again referring the disagreeable decision to his own tribunal. Feeling himself obliged in his quality of judge to give this decision, he sought to placate the Jews in different ways. One of these was a private interview with some of the servants and friends of the high priests and priests. He urged them to prevail upon their masters and friends, not any more to ask for the release of the malefactor Barabbas, but instead demand the release of our Redeemer; and to be satisfied with some punishment he was willing to administer before setting Him free. This measure Pilate had taken before they arrived a second time to press their demand for a sentence upon Jesus. The proposal to choose between freeing either Barabbas or Jesus was made to the Jews, not only once, but two or three times. The first time before sending Him to Herod and the second time after his return; this is related by the Evangelists with some variation, though not essentially contradicting truth (Matthew 27, 17). Pilate spoke to the Jews and said: "You have brought this Man before me, accusing Him of perverting the people by his doctrines; and having examined Him in your presence, I was not convinced of the truth of your accusations. And Herod, to whom I have sent Him and before whom you repeated your accusations, refused to condemn Him to death. It will be sufficient to correct and chastise Him for the present, in order that He may amend. As I am to release some malefactor for the feast of the Pasch, I will release Christ, if you will have Him freed, and punish Barabbas." But the multitude of the Jews, thus informed how much Pilate desired to set Jesus free, shouted with one voice: "Enough, enough, not Christ, but Barabbas deliver unto us."

The custom of giving freedom to an imprisoned criminal at this great solemnity of the Pasch was introduced by the Jews in grateful remembrance of the release of their forefathers from servitude by their passage through the Red Sea, when the Almighty freed them from the power of Pharao by killing the firstborn children of the Egyptians and afterwards annihilating him and his armies in the waters of the Red sea (Exodus 12, 29). In gratitude for this favor the Jews always sought out the greatest malefactor and pardoned him his crimes; while they refused such clemency to those who were less guilty. In their treaties with the Romans they expressly reserved this privilege; and the governors complied with it. But in the present instance they failed to follow out in their demands what they were so loudly proclaiming in regard to Jesus. According to law they were to demand the release of the greatest criminal and this they proclaimed Jesus to be; yet they persisted in demanding the punishment of Christ and the release of Barabbas, whom they judged less guilty. In such blindness and perversity had the wrath and envy of the demon cast them, that they lost the light of reason even in their own affairs and against their own selves.

While Pilate was thus disputing with the Jews in the pretorium, his wife, Procula, happened to hear of his doings and she sent him a message telling him: "What hast thou to do with this Man? Let him go free; for I warn thee that I have had this very day some visions in regard to Him!" This warning of Procula originated through the activity of Lucifer and his demons. For they, observing all that was happening in regard to the person of Christ and the unchangeable patience with which He bore all injuries, were more and more confused and staggered in their rabid fury. Although the swollen pride of Lucifer could not explain how his Divinity could ever subject Itself to such great insults, nor how He could permit his body to suffer such ill-treatment, and although he could not come to any certain conviction, whether this Jesus was a God-man or not; yet the dragon was persuaded, that some great mystery was here transpiring among men which would be the cause of great damage and defeat to him and his malice if he did not succeed in arresting its progress in the world. Having come to this conclusion with his demons, he many times suggested to the pharisees the propriety of ceasing their persecutions of Christ. These suggestions, however, since they originated from malice and were void of any power for good, failed to move the obstinate and perverted hearts of the Jews. Despairing of success the demons betook themselves to the wife of Pilate and spoke to her in dreams, representing to her that this Man was just and without guilt, that if her husband should sentence Him he would be deprived of his rank and she herself would meet with great adversity. They urged her to advise Pilate to release Jesus and punish Barabbas, if she did not wish to draw misfortune upon their house and their persons.

Procula was filled with great fear and terror at these visions, and as soon as she heard what was passing between the Jews and her husband, she sent him the message mentioned by saint Matthew, not to meddle with this Man nor condemn One to death, whom she held to be just. The demon also injected similar misgivings into the mind of Pilate and these warnings of his wife only increased them. Yet, as all his considerations rested upon worldly policy, and as he had not cooperated with the true helps given him by the Savior, all these fears retarded his unjust proceedings only so long as no other more powerful consideration arose, as will be seen in effect. But just now he began for the third time to argue (as saint Luke tells us), insisting upon the innocence of Christ our Lord and that he found no crime in Him nor any guilt worthy of death, and therefore he would punish and then dismiss Him (Luke 23,22). As we shall see in the next chapter, he did really punish Christ in order to see whether the Jews would be satisfied. But the Jews, on the contrary, demanded that Christ be crucified. Thereupon Pilate asked for water and released Barabbas. Then he washed his hands in the presence of all the people, saying: "I have no share in the death of this just Man, whom you condemn. Look to yourselves in what you are doing, for I wash my hands in order that you may understand they are not sullied in the blood of the Innocent." Pilate thought that by this ceremony he could excuse himself entirely and that he thereby could put its blame upon the princes of the Jews and upon the people who demanded it. The wrath of the Jews was so blind and foolish that for the satisfaction of seeing Jesus crucified, they entered upon this agreement with Pilate and took upon themselves and upon their children the responsibility for this crime. Loudly proclaiming this terrible sentence and curse, they exclaimed: "His blood come upon us and upon our children" (Matthew 27, 25).

O most foolish and cruel blindness! O inconceivable rashness! The unjust condemnation of the Just and the blood of the Innocent, whom the judge himself is forced to proclaim guiltless, you wish to take upon yourselves and upon your children, in order that his blood may call out against you to the end of the world! O perfidious and sacrilegious Jews! So lightly then weighs the blood of the Lamb, who bears the sins of the world, and the life of a Man, who is at the same time God! How is it possible you wish to load with it yourselves and your children? If He had been only your brother, your benefactor and master, your audacity would have been tremendous and your malice execrable. Justly indeed do you merit the punishment which you meet; and that the burden, which you have put upon yourselves and your children, allows you no rest or relief in all the world: it is just that this burden should rest upon you heavier than heaven and earth. But, alas! Though this divine Blood was intended to wash and cleanse all the children of Adam, and though it was in effect poured out upon all the children of the holy Church, yet there are many belonging to it who make themselves guilty of this blood by their works in the same manner as the Jews charged themselves with it, both by word and deed. They did not know or believe that it was the blood of the Savior, while Catholics both know and confess that it is their Redeemer's.

The sins and depraved lives of the Christians proclaim louder than tongues their abuse of the blood of Christ and their consent to the guilt in his death which they load upon themselves. Let Christ be affronted, spit upon, buffeted, stretched upon a cross, despised, let Him yield to Barabbas and die; let Him be tormented, scourged and crowned with thorns for our sins: let his blood interest us no more than that it flow copiously and be imputed to us for all eternity: let the incarnate God suffer and die; if only we are left free to enjoy the apparent goods of this world, to seize the pleasing hour, to use creatures for our comfort, to be crowned with roses, live in joy; let our power be unrefrained, let no one seek preference before us; be we permitted to despise hwnility, abhor poverty, hoard up riches. engage in all deceits, forgive no injuries. entertain the delights of carnal pleasures. let our eyes see nothing that they shall not covet. Such be our rule in life without regard for aught else. And if by all this we crucify Christ, let his blood come upon us and upon our children.

Ask the damned in hell. whether these were not the sentiments expressed in their works as described by Solomon, and whether it was not because they spoke thus foolishly in their hearts, that they were called impious. and were so in reality. What else except damnation can they expect, who abuse the blood of Christ and waste it upon themselves. not as such who are seeking a remedy? Where do we find, among the children of the Church. anyone that would willingly pennit a thief and malefactor to be preferred to him? So little is this doctrine of humility practiced, that one excites surprise if he allows another just as good and honorable as himself, or even more honorable, to take precedence. Though it is certain that no one can be found as good as Christ or liS bad as Barabbas. yet there are innumerable men who. in spite of this example. are offended and judge themselves disgraced. if they are not preferred and exalted by honors. riches and dignities, and in whatever pertains to the ostentation and applause of the world. These are sought after. contended for and solicited; in such things are consumed the thoughts and all the exertions and powers of men, almost from the time in which they can use their faculties until they lose them. The most lamentable misfortune is, that even those who. by their profession and their state. have renounced and turned their backs upon such things, do not free themselves. While the Savior has commanded them to forget their people and the house of their parents (Psalms 44, 11), they devote to them the best part of their human existence, by giving them their attention and solicitude in the direction of their affairs, their best wishes and care in the augmentation of their worldly goods. It seems but a small matter to them to engage themselves in these vanities. Instead of forgetting the house of their father they forget the house of their God in which they live, and where they are divinely assisted to gain a salvation, an honor and esteem never possible in the world, and where they receive their sustenance without any anxiety or worry. They show themselves ungrateful for all these benefits by dri fting away from the humility due to their state. Thus the humility of Christ our Savior, his patience, his injuries, the dishonor of the cross, the imitation of Christ's works, the following of his doctrines; all is left to the poor, to the lonely ones, to the weak and humble of this world; while the ways of Sion are deserted and full of wailing, because there are so few who will come to the solemn feast of the imitation of Christ our Lord (Lamentations 1,4).

Pilate was not conscious of the absurdity of his pretense, that to have washed his hands and to have charged the Jews with the blood of Christ, was sufficient to clear him before his conscience and before men; for by this ceremony, so full of hypocrisy and deceit, he tried to satisfy both. It is true that the Jews were the principal actors and more guilty in the condemnation of the innocent God-man, and that they themselves expressly charged themselves with its guilt. But Pilate was not on that account free from it; since, knowing the innocence of Christ our Lord, he should not have allowed a thief and robber to be preferred before Christ; neither should he have chastised, nor pretended to correct Him, who showed nothing that could be corrected or amended (Luke 23, 25). Much less should he have condemned and delivered Him over to his mortal enemies, whose envy and cruelty was so evident. He is not a just judge who is aware of the truth and justice and places it in the balance with his own human respect and his own personal interest; for such a course drags down the right reason of men who are so cowardly of heart. Since they do not possess the strength and perfection of mind necessary to a judge, they cannot resist their greed, or their human respect. In their blind passions they forsake justice in order not to endanger their temporal advantages, as happened to Pilate.

In the house of Pilate, through the ministry of the holy angels, our Queen was placed in such a position that She could hear the disputes of the iniquitous judge with the scribes and priests concerning the innocence of Christ our Savior, and concerning the release of Barabbas in preference to Him. All the clamors of these human tigers She heard in silence and admirable meekness, as the living counterpart of her most holy Son. Although She preserved the unchanging propriety and modesty of her exterior, all the malicious words of the Jews pierced her sorrowful heart like a twoedged sword. But the voices of her unspoken sorrows resounded in the ears of the eternal Father more pleasantly and sweetly than the lamentation of the beautiful Rachel who, as Jeremias says, was beweeping her children because they cannot be restored (Jeremias 31, 15). Our most beautiful Rachel the purest Mary, sought not revenge, but pardon for her enemies, who were depriving Her of the Only-begotten of the Father and her only Son. She imitated all the actions of the most holy Soul of Christ and accompanied Him in the works of most exalted holiness and perfection; for neither could her torments hinder her charity, nor her affliction diminish her fervor, nor could the tumult distract her attention, nor the outrageous injuries of the multitudes prevent her interior recollection: under all circumstances She practiced the most exalted virtues in the most eminent degree.

Instruction, which Mary, the Queen of Heaven Gave Me

My daughter, in what thou hast written and understood, I see thee astonished to find, that Pilate and Herod exhibited less unkindness and cruelty in the death of my divine Son than the priests, high priests and pharisees; and thou dwellest much upon the fact that those were secular and genTHE judges, while these were teachers of the law and priests of the people of Israel, professing the true faith. In answer to thy thoughts I will remind thee of a doctrine not new, which thou hast understood on former occasions; but I wish that thou refresh it in thy mind and remember it for the rest of thy life. Know then, my dearest, that a fall from the highest position is extremely dangerous and the damage done is either irreparable, or very difficult of redress. Lucifer held an eminent position in heaven, as regards both natural gifts and gifts of grace; for in beauty he excelled all the creatures, and by his sin he fell to the deepest abyss of loathsomeness and misery and into a more hardened obstinacy than all his followers. The first parents of the human race, Adam and Eve, were exalted to the highest dignity and raised to exquisite favor, as coming forth from the hand of the Almighty: their fall caused perdition to themselves and to all their posterity, and faith teaches what was the cost of their salvation. To restore them and their posterity was the work of an infinite mercy.

Many other souls have reached the heights of perfection and have thence fallen most unfortunately, arriving at a state in which they almost despaired or found themselves incapable of rising. This sad state in the creature originates from many causes. The first is the dismay and boundless confusion of one who feels that he has fallen from an exalted state of virtue; mr he knows that he has not only lost great blessings, but he does not expect to obtain greater ones than those of the past and those he has lost; nor does he promise himself more finnness in keeping those he can obtain through renewed efforts, than he has shown in those acquired and now lost through his ingratitude. From this dangerous distrust originates lukewarmness. want of fervor and diligence. absence of zeal and devotion; since diffidence extinguishes all these in the soul. just as the sprightliness of ardent hope overcomes many difficulties. strengthens and vivifies weak human creatures to undertake great works. Another obstacle there Isaias not less formidable, namely: the souls accustomed to the blessings of God, either through their office, as the priests and religious. or by the exercise of virtues and the abundance of divine favors. as spiritual minded persons, usually aggravate their sins by a certain contempt of these very blessings and a certain abuse of the divine things. For by the abundance of the divine favors they fall into a dangerous dullness of mind. They begin to think little of the divine favors and become irreverent. Thus failing to cooperate with God's grace, they hinder ts effect. They lose the grace of holy fear of the Lord. Which arouses and stimulates the will to obey the divine commandments and to be alert in the avoidance of sin and pursuit of eternal life in the friendship of God. This is an evident danger for lukewarm priests, who frequent the holy Eucharist and other Sacraments, without fear and reverence; also for the learned and wise, and the powerful of this world, who so reluctantly correct and amend their lives. They have lost the appreciation and veneration of the remedial helps of the Church, namely, the Sacraments, preaching and instruction. Thus these medicines, which for other sinners are so salutary and counteract ignorance, weaken those who are the physicians of the spiritual life.

There are other reasons for this kind of danger, which must be referred to the Lord himself. For the sins of those souls who, by their state or by their advanced virtues, are more closely bound to their God, are weighed in the balance of God's justice in quite a different way from the sins of those who have been less favored by his mercy. Although the sins of all are more or less essentially the same, yet the circumstances of sin are very different. For the priests and teachers, the powerful and the dignitaries, and those who, on account of their station or by reputation, are supposed to be advanced in a holy life, cause great scandal by their' fall or by any sins they commit. There is much morel of bold disrespect in their presumption and temerity, against God, whom they know better and to whom they owe much more, but whom they offend with more deliberation and knowledge than the ignorant. Hence, as isl evident from the tenor of all the holy Scriptures, the sins of Catholics, and especially of those that are instructed and enlightened, are so displeasing to God. As the term of each man's life is preordained for each one as the time in which he is to gain the eternal reward, so the measure or number of sins to be borne by the patience or forbearance of the Lord is likewise preordained. This measure of divine justice is determined not only by the number and quantity of the sins, but also by their quality and weight. Thus it may happen, that in the souls favored by greater enlightenment and graces of heaven, the grievousness supplies what is wanting in the number of the sins, and that with fewer sins they are forsaken sooner and chastised more severely than others with many more sins. Nor can all expect for themselves the same issue as David (II Kings 12, 13) and saint Peter; because not all of them have to their credit as many good actions to be remembered by the Lord. Besides the special privileges of some cannot be set up as a rule for all others; because, according to the secret judgments of the Lord, not all are destined for a special office.

By this explanation, my dearest, thou wilt be able to satisfy thy doubts and thou wilt understand what a bitter evil so many souls incur, whom the Almighty has redeemed by his blood, placed in the way of light and drawn toward Himself: and how some persons can fall from a more exalted state into more perverse obstinacy than others below them in station. This truth is well illustrated in the mystery of my Son's Passion, in which the priests, scribes and the whole people were much more indebted to their God than the heathens, who knew not of the true religion. I desire that this truth, as !xhibited by their example, convince thee of this terrible anger and excite in thee holy fear. And with this fear oin humble thanks and an exalted esteem of the favors of the Lord. In the days of abundance, be not unmind'ul of the hour of want (Ecclesiaticus 13, 25). Ponder as well he one as the other within thyself, and remember that thou carriest thy treasure in a fragile vessel, which thou canst easily lose (II Corinthians 4, 7). Know well, that the reception of such blessings argues not merit, and the possession of them is not due to thee in justice, but comes to thee by liberality and kindness. That the Most High has favored thee with so much familiar intercourse is no assurance that thou canst not fall, and no license to live carelessly and without reverence and fear. All things happen to thee according to the number and greatness of thy blessings; for the wrath of the serpent has increased toward thee in proportion, and is more alert against thee than against other souls. He has become aware that the Most High has not been so liberally loving to men of many generations as toward thee, and if thou I meet so many blessings and mercies with ingratitude, . thou shalt be most wretched and worthy of a rigorous . punishment, against which thou canst make no objection.

Our Savior Is Scourged

Our Savior, by order of Pilate, is scourged, crowned with thorns and mocked. The bahavior of this most most holy Mary during this time

Pilate, aware of the obstinate hostility of the Jews against Jesus of Nazareth, and unwilling to condemn Him to death, of which he knew Him to be innocent, thought that a severe scourging of Jesus might placate the fury of the ungrateful people and soothe the envy of the priests and the scribes. If He should have failed in anything pertaining to their ceremonies and rites, they would probably consider Him sufficiently chastised and cease in their persecutions and in their clamors for his Death. Pilate was led to this belief by what they had told him in the course of his trial; for they had vainly and foolishly calumniated Christ of not obser.·ing t~e sabbath and other ceremonies, as is evident from his sermons reported by the Evangelists (John 9, 6). But Pilate was entirely wrong in his judgment and acted like an ignorant man; for neither could the Master of all holiness be guilty of any defect in the observance of that Law, which He had come not to abolish but to fulfill (Matthew 5, 7) ; nor even if the accusation had been true, would He have deserved such an outrageous punishment. For the laws of the Jews, far from demanding such an inhuman and cruel scourging, contained other regulations for atonement of the more common faults. In still greater error was this judge in expecting any mercy or natural kindness and compassion from the Jews. Their anger and wrath against the most meek Master was not human, not such as ordinarily is appeased by the overthrow and humiliation of the enemy. For men have hearts of flesh, and the love of their own kind is natural and the source of at least some compassion. But these perfidious Jews were clothed in the guise of demons, or rather transformed into demons, who exert the more furious rage against those who are rendered more helpless and wretched; who, when they see anyone most helpless, say: let us pursue him now, since he has none to defend nor free him from our hands.

Such was the implacable fury of the priests and of their confederates, the pharisees, against the Author of life. For Lucifer, despairing of being able to hinder his murder by the Jews, inspired them with his own dreadful malice and outrageous cruelty. Pilate. placed between the known truth and his human and terrestrial considerations, chose to follow the erroneous leading of the latter, and order Jesus to be severely scourged. though he had himself declared Him free from guilt (John 19, 1). Thereupon those ministers of satan, with many others, brought Jesus our Savior to the place of punishment, which was a courtyard or enclosure attached to the house and set apart for the torture of criminals in order to force them to confess their crimes. It was enclosed by a low, open building, surrounded by columns, some of which supported the roof, while others were lower and stood free. To one of these columns, which was of marble, they bound Jesus very securely; for they still thought Him a magician and feared his escape.

They first took off the white garment with not less ignominy than when they clothed Him therein in the house of the adulterous homicide Herod. In loosening the ropes and chains, which He had borne since his capture in the garden, they cruelly widened the wounds which his bonds had made in his arms and wrists. Having freed his hands, they commanded Him with infamous blasphemies to despoil Himself of the seamless tunic which He wore. This was the identical garment with which his most blessed Mother had clothed Him in Egypt when He first began to walk, as I have related in its place. Our Lord at present had no other garment, since they had taken from Him his mantle, or cloak, when they seized Him in the garden. The Son of the eternal Father obeyed the executioners and began to unclothe Himself, ready to bear the shame of the exposure of his most sacred and modest body before such a multitude of people. But his tormentors, impatient at the delay which modesty required, tore away the tunic with violence in order to hasten his undressing and, as is said, flay the sheep with the wool. With the exception of a strip of cloth for a cincture, which He wore beneath the tunic and with which his Mother likewise had clothed Him in Egypt, the Lord stood now naked. These garments had grown with his sacred body, nor hac! He ever taken them off. The same is to be said of his shoes, which his Mother had placed on his feet. However. as I have said on a former occasion, He had many times walked barefooted during his preaching.

I understand that some of the doctors have said or have persuaded themselves, that our Savior Jesus at his scourging and at his crucifixion, for his greater humiliation, permitted the executioners to despoil Him of all his clothing. But having again been commanded under holy obedience to ascertain the truth in this matter, I was told that the divine Master was prepared to suffer all the insults compatible with decency; that the executioners attempted to subject his body to this shame of total nakedness, seeking to despoil Him of the cincture, which covered his loins; but in that they failed; because, on touching it, their arms became paralyzed and stiff, as had happened also in the house of Caiphas, when they attempted to take off his clothes. All the six of his tormentors separately made the attempt with the same result. Yet afterwards, these ministers of evil. in order to scourge Him with greater effect, raised some of the coverings; for so much the Lord permitted, but not that He should be uncovered and despoiled of his garments entirely. The miracle of their being hindered and paralyzed in their brutal attempts did not, however, move or soften the hearts of these human beasts; but in their diabolical insanity they attributed it all to the supposed sorcery and witchcraft of the Author of truth and life.

Thus the Lord stood uncovered in the presence of a great multitude and the six torturers bound Him brutally to one of the columns in order to chastise Him' so much the more at their ease. Then, two and two at a time, they began to scourge Him with such inhuman cruelty, as was possible only in men possessed by Lucifer, as were these executioners. The first two scourged the innocent Savior with hard and thick cords, full of rough, knots, and in their sacrilegious fury strained all the powers of their body to inflict the blows. This first scourging raised in the deified body of the Lord great welts and, livid tumors, so that the sacred blood gathered beneath the skin and disfigured his entire body. Already it began to ooze through the wounds. The first two having at length desisted, the second pair continued the scourging in still greater emulation; with hardened leather thongs they leveled their strokes upon the places already sore and caused the discolored tumors to break open and shed forth the sacred blood until it bespattered and drenched the garments of the sacrilegious torturers, running down also in streams to the pavement. Those two gave way to the third pair of scourgers, who commenced to beat the Lord with extremely tough rawhides, dried hard like osier twigs. They scourged Him stil\ more cruelly, because they were wounding, not so much his virginal body, as cutting into the wounds already produced by the previous scourging. Besides they had been secretly incited to greater fury by the demons, who were filled with new rage at the patience of Christ.

As the veins of the sacred body had now been opened and his whole Person seemed but one continued wound, the third pair found no more room for new wounds. Their ceaseless blows inhumanly tore the immaculate and virginal flesh of Christ our Redeemer and scattered many pieces of it about the pavement; so much so that a large portion of the shoulderbones were exposed and showed red through the flowing blood; in other places also the bones were laid bare larger than the palm of the hand. In order to wipe out entirely that beauty, which exceeded that of all other men (Psalms 44, 3), they beat Him in the face and in the feet and hands, thus leaving unwounded not a single spot in which they conld exert their fury and wrath against the most innocent Lamb. The divine blood flowed to the ground, gathering here and there in great abundance. The scourging in the face, and in the hands and feet, was unspeakably painful, because these parts are so full of sensitive and delicate nerves. His venerable countenance became so swollen and wounded that the blood and the swellings blinded Him. In addition to their blows the executioners spirted upon his Person their disgusting spittle and loaded Him with insulting epithets (Lamentations 3, 30). The exact number of blows dealt out to the Savior from head to foot was 5,115. The great Lord and Author of all creation who, by his divine nature was incapable of suffering, was, in his human flesh and for our sake, reduced to a man of sorrows as prophesied, and was made to experience our infirmities, becoming the last of men (Isaias 53, 3), a man of sorrows and the outcast of the people.

The multitudes who had followed the Lord, filled up the courtyard of Pilate's house and the surrounding streets; for all of them waited for the issue of this event, discussing and arguing about it according to each one's views. Amid all this confusion the Virgin Mother endured unheard of insults, and She was deeply afflicted by the injuries and blasphemies heaped upon her divine Son by the Jews and gentiles. When they brought Jesus to the scourging place She retired in the company of the Marys and saint John to a corner of the courtyard. Assisted by her divine visions, She there witnessed all the scourging and the torments of our Savior. Although She did not see it with the eyes of her body nothing was hidden to Her, no more than if She had been standing quite near. Human thoughts cannot comprehend how great and how diverse were the afflictions and sorrows of the great Queen and Mistress of the angels: together with many other mysteries of the Divinity they shall become manifest in the next life, for the glory of the Son and Mother. I have already mentioned in other places of this history, and especially in that of the Passion, that the blessed Mother felt in her own body all the torments of her Son. This was true also of the scourging, which She felt in all the parts of her virginal body, in the same intensity as they were felt by Christ in his body. Although She shed no blood except what flowed from her eyes with her tears, nor was lacerated in her flesh; yet the bodily pains so changed and disfigured Her, that saint John and the holy women failed to find in Her any resemblance of Herself. Resides the tortures of the body She suffered ineffable sorrows of the soul; there sorrow was augmented in proportion to the immensity of her insight (Ecclesiastes 1, 18). For her sorrows flowed not only from the natural love of a mother and a supreme love of Christ as her God, but it was proportioned to her power of judging more accurately than all creatures of the innocence of Christ, the dignity of his divine Person, the atrocity of the insults coming from the perfidious Jews and the children of Adam, whom He was freeing from eternal death.

Having at length executed the sentence of scourging, the executioners unbound the Lord from the column, and with imperious and blasphemous presumption commanded Him immediately to put on his garment. But while they had scourged the most meek Master, one of his tormentors, instigated by the devil, had hidden his clothes out of sight. in order to prolong the nakedness and exposure of his divine Person for their derision and sport. This evil purpose suggested by the devil. was well known to the Mother of the Lord. She therefore, making use of her power as Queen, commanded Lucifer and all his demons to leave the neighborhood, and immediately, compelled by her sovereign power and virtue, they fled. She gave orders that the tunic be brought by the holy angels within reach of her most holy Son, so that He could again cover his sacred and lacerated body. All this was immediately attended to, although the sacrilegious executioners understood not the miracle, nor how it had been wrought; they attributed it all to the sorcery and magic of the demon. During this protracted nakedness our Savior had. in addition to his wounds, suffered greatly from the cold of that morning as mentioned by the Evangelists (Mark 14, 55; Luke 22, 35; John 18, 18). His sacred blood had frozen and compressed the wounds, which had become inflamed and extremely painful; the cold had diminished his powers of resistance, although the fire of his infinite charity strained them to the utmost in order to suffer more and more. Though compassion is so natural in rational creatures, there was none for Him in his affliction and necessity, except that of his sorrowful Mother, who tearfully bewailed and pitied Him in the name of the whole human race.

Among other divine mysteries, hidden to the wise of this world, this also causes great astonishment, that the wrath of the Jews, who were men of flesh and blood like ourselves, should not have been appeased at their seeing Christ torn and wounded by 5,115 lashes; that the sight of a person so lacerated should not have moved their natural compassion. but should arouse their envy to inflict new and unheard of tortures upon the Victim. Their implacable fury at once planned another outrageous cruelty. They went to Pilate and in the presence of his counselors said: "This seducer and deceiver of the people, Jesus of Nazareth, in his boasting and vanity, has sought to be recognized by all as the king of the Jews. In order that his pride may be humbled and his presumption be confounded. we desire your permission to place upon Him the royal insignia merited by his fantastic pretensions." Pilate yielded to the unjust demand of the Jews, permitting them to proceed according to their intentions.

Thereupon they took Jesus to the pretorium, where, with the same cruelty and contempt, they again despoiled him of his garments and in order to deride Him before all the people as a counterfeit king, clothed Him in a much torn and soiled mantle of purple color. They placed also upon his sacred head a cap made of woven thorns, to serve Him as a crown (John 19, 2). This cap was woven of thorn branches and in such a manner that many of the hard and sharp thorns would penetrate into the skull, some of them to the ears and others to the eyes. Hence one of the greatest tortures suffered by the Lord was that of the c;own of thorns. Instead of a sceptre they placed into his hands a contemptible reed. They also threw over His shoulders a violet colored mantle, something of the style of capes worn in churches; for such a garment belonged to the vestiture of a king. In this array of a mockking the perfidious Jews decked out Him, who by his nature and by every right was the King of kings and the Lord of lords (Apocalypse 19, 16). Then all the soldiers, in the presence of the priests and pharisees, gathered around Him and heaped upon Him their blasphemous mockery and derision. Some of them bent their knees and mockingly said to Him: God save Thee, King of the Jews. Others buffeted Him; others snatched the cane from his hands and struck Him on his crowned head; others ejected their disgusting spittle upon Him; all of them. instigated by furious demons. insulted and affronted Him in different manners.

O charity incomprehensible and exceeding all measure! O patience never seen or imagined among mortals! Who, O my Lord and God, since Thou art the true and mighty God both in essence and in thy works, who could oblige Thee to suffer the humiliation of such unheard of torments, insults and blasphemies? On the contrary, O my God, who among men has not done many things which offend Thee and which should have caused Thee to refuse suffering and to deny them thy favor? Who could ever believe all this, if we knew not of thy

.

infinite goodness. But now, since we see it and in firm faith look upon such admirable blessings and miracles of love, where is our judgment? what effect upon us has the light of truth? What enchantment is this that we suffer, since at the very sight of thy sorrows, scourges, thorns, insults and affronts, we seek for ourselves, without the least shame or fear, the delights, the riches, the ease, the preferments and vanities of this world? Truly, great is the number of fools (Ecclesiastes 1, 15), since the greatest foolishness and dishonesty is to recognize a debt and be unwilling to pay it; to receive blessings and never give thanks for them; to have before one's eyes the greater good, and despise it; to claim it for ourselves and make no use of it; to turn away and fly from life, and seek eternal death. The most innocent Jesus opened not his mouth in those great and many injuries. Nor was the furious wrath of the Jews appeased, either by the mockery and derision of the divine Master, or by the torments added to the contempt of his most exalted Person.

It seemed to Pilate that the spectacle of a man so ill-treated as Jesus of Nazareth would move and fill with shame the hearts of that ungrateful people. He therefore commanded Jesus to be brought from the pretorium to an open window, where all could see Him crowned with thorns, disfigured by the scourging and the ignominious vestiture of a mocking. Pilate himself spoke to the people, calling out to them: "Ecce Homo," "Behold, what a man!" (John 19, 5). See this Man, whom you hold as your enemy! What more can I do with Him than to have punished Him in this severe manner? You certainly have nothing more to fear from Him. I do not find any cause of death in Him. What this judge said was certainly the full truth; but in his own words he condemned his outrageous injustice, since, knowing and confessing that this Man was just and not guilty of death, he had nevertheless ordered Him to be tormented and punished in such a way that. according to the natural course. he should have been killed many times over. O blindness of self-love! O hellish malice of estimating only the influence of those, who can confer or take away mere earthly dignities! How deeply do such motives obscure the reason, how much do they twist the course of justice, how completely do they pervert the greatest truths in judging of the just by the standards of the unjust! Tremble, ye judges of the earth (Psalms 2. 10), look to it that the sentences you render are not full of deceit; for you yourselves shall be judged and condemned by your unjust judgments! As the priests and pharisees, in their eager and insatiable hostility, were irrevocably bent upon taking away the life of Christ our Savior, nothing but his Death would content or satisfy them; therefore they answered Pilate: "Crucify Him, Crucify Him!" (John 19,6.)

When the Blessed among women, most holy Mary. saw her divine Son as Pilate showed Him to the people and heard him say: "Ecce homo!" She fell upon her knees and openly adored Him as the true God-man. The same was also done by saint John and the holy women, together with all the holy angels of the Queen and Lady; for they saw that not only Mary, as the Mother of the Savior, but that God himself desired them thus to act. The most prudent Lady spoke to the eternal Father, to the angels and especially to her most beloved Son precious words of sorrow, compassion and profound reverence, possible to be conceived only in her chaste and love inflamed bosom. In her exalted wisdom She pondered also the ways and means by which the evidences of his innocence could be made most opportunely manifest at a time when He was so insulted, mocked and despised by the Jews. With this most proper intention She renewed the petitions above mentioned, namely, that Pilate, in his quality of judge, continue to maintain the innocence of Jesus our Redeemer and that all the world should understand, that Jesus was not guilty of death nor of any of the crimes imputed to Him by the Jews.

On account of these prayers of the most blessed Mother Pilate was made to feel great compassion at seeing Jesus so horribly scourged and ill-treated and regret at having punished Him so severely. Although he was naturally disposed to such emotions by his soft and compassionate disposition; yet they were principally caused by the light he received through the intercession of the Queen and Mother of grace. This same light moved the unjust judge after the crowning of thorns to prolong his parley with the Jews for the release of Christ, as is recorded in the nineteenth chapter of the Gospel of saint John. When they again asked him to crucify the Lord, he answered: "Take Him yourselves and crucify Him, for I do not find any cause for doing it." They replied: "According to our law He is guilty of death, for He claims to be the Son of God." This reply threw Pilate into greater consternation, for he conceived it might be true, that Jesus was the Son of God according to his heathen notions of the Divinity. Therefore he withdrew with Jesus into the pretorium, where, speaking with Him alone, he asked whence He was? The Lord did not answer this question; for Pilate was not in a state of mind either to understand or to merit a reply. Nevertheless he insisted and said to the King of heaven: "Dost Thou then not speak to me? Dost Thou not know, that I have power to crucify Thee and power to dismiss Thee?" Pilate sought to move Him to defend Himself and tell what he wanted to know. It seemed to Pilate that a man so wretched and tormented would gladly accept any offer of favor from a judge.

But the Master of truth answered Pilate without defending Himself but with unexpected dignity; for He said: "Thou shouldst not have any power against Me, unless it were given thee from above. Therefore, he that hath delivered Me to thee, hath the greater sin." This answer by itself made the condemnation of Christ inexcusable in Pilate; since he could have understood therefrom, that neither he nor Caesar had any power of jurisdiction over this man Jesus; that by a much higher decree He had been so unreasonably and unjustly delivered over to his judgment; that therefore Judas and the priests had committed a greater sin than he in not releasing Him; and that nevertheless He too was guilty of the same crime. though not in such high degree. Pilate failed to arrive at these mysterious truths; but he was struck with still greater consternation at the words of Christ our Lord, and therefore made still more strenuous efforts to liberate Him. The priests, who were now abundantly aware of his intentions, threatened him with he displeasure of the emperor, which he would incur, if he permitted this One, who had aspired to be king, to cape death. They said: "If thou freest this Man, thou no friend of Caesar; since he who makes a king of himself rises up against his orders and commands." They rged this because the Roman emperors never permitted anyone in the whole empire to assume the title or insignia f a King without their consent and order; if therefore Pilate should permit it, he would contravene the decrees of Caesar. He was much disturbed at this malicious and threatening intimation of the Jews, and seating himself in his tribunal at the sixth hour in order to pass sentence upon the Lord, he once more turned to plead with the Jews, saying: "See there your King!" And all of them answered: "Away with Him, away with Him, crucify Him!" He replied: "Shall I crucify your King?" Whereupon they shouted unanimously: "We have no other king than Caesar."

Pilate permitted himself to be overcome by the obstinacy and malice of the Jews. On the day of Parasceve then, seated in his tribunal, which in Greek was called Iithostratos, and in Hebrew gabatha, he pronounced the sentence of death against the Author of life, as I shall relate in the following chapter. The Jews departed from the hall in great exultation and joy, proclaiming the sentence of the most innocent Lamb. That they did not realize whom they thus sought to annihilate was the occasion of our Redemption. All this was well known to the sorrowful Mother, who, though outside of the hall of judgment, sawall the proceedings by exalted vision. When the priests and pharisees rushed forth exulting in the condemnation of Christ to the death of the Cross, the pure heart of this most blessed Mother was filled with new sorrow and was pierced and transfixed with the sword of unalleviated bitterness. Since the sorrow of most holy Mary on this occasion surpassed all that can enter the thoughts of man, it is useless to speak more of it, and it must be referred to the pious meditation of Christians. Just as impossible is it to enumerate her interior acts of adoration, worship, reverence, love, compassion, sorrow and resignation.

Instruction, which Mary, the Queen of Heaven Gave Me

My daughter, thou reftectest with wonder upon the hardness and malice of the Jews, the weakness of Pilate, who knew of their evil dispositions and permitted himself to be overcome, though fully convinced of the innocence of my Son and Lord. I wish to relieve thee of this astonishment by furnishing thee with instructions and warnings suitable for making thee careful on the path to eternal life. Know then that the ancient prophecies concerning the mysteries of the Redemption and all the holy Scriptures were to be infallibly fulfilled; for sooner shall heaven and earth fall to pieces, than that their words fail of their effect as determined in the divine Mind (Matthew 24, 35; Acts 3, 18). In order that the most ignominious death foretold for my Lord should be brought about (Sap. 2, 20; Jeremias 11, 19) it was necessary that He should be persecuted by men. But that these men should happen to be the Jews, the priests and the unjust Pilate, was their own misfortune, not the choice of the Almighty, who wishes to save all (I Timothy 2, 4). Their own wickedness and malice brought them to their ruin; for they resisted the great grace of having in their midst their Redeemer and Master, of :mowing Him, of conversing with Him, of hearing his :Ioctrine and preaching, of witnessing his miracles; and :hey had received such great favors, as none of the ancient Patriarchs had attained by all their longings (Matthew 13,7). Hence the cause of the Savior was justified. He manifestly had cultivated his vineyard by his own hands and showered his favors upon it (Matthew 21, 33). But it brought Him only thorns and briars, and its keepers took away his life, refusing to recognize Him, as was heir opportunity and their duty before all other men.

This same, which happened in the head Christ the Lord and Son of God, must happen to all the members of his mystical body, that is, to the just and predestined to the end of the world. For it would be monstrous to see the members incongruous with the Head, the children show no relation with the Father, or the disciples unlike their Master. Although sinners must always exist (Matthew 18, 7), since in this world the just shan always be mingled with the unjust, the predestined with the reprobate, the persecutors with the persecuted, the murderers with the murdered, the afflicting with the afflicted; yet these lots are decided by the malice and the goodness of men. Unhappy shall be he, through whom scandal comes into the world and who thus makes himself an instrument of the demon. This kind of activity was begun in the new Church by the priests and pharisees, and by Pilate, who an persecuted the Head of this mystic body and, in the further course of the world, by all those who persecute its members, the saints and the predestined, imitating and following the Jews and the devil in their evil work.

Think, then, my dearest, which of these lots thou wishest to choose in the sight of my Son and me. If thou seest thy Redeemer, thy Spouse and thy Chief tormented, afflicted, crowned with thorns and saturated with reproaches and at the same time desirest to have a part in Him and be a member of his mystical body, it is not becoming, or even possible, that thou live steeped in the pleasures of the flesh. Thou must be the persecuted and not a persecutor, the oppressed and not the oppressor; the one that bears the cross, that encounters the scandal, and not that gives it; the one that suffers, and at the same time makes none of the neighbors suffer. On the contrary, thou must exert thyself for their conversion and salvation in as far as is compatible with the perfection of thy state and vocation. This is the portion of the friends of God and the inheritance of his children in mortal life; in this consists the participation in grace and glory, which by His torments and reproaches and by his death of the Cross my Son and Lord has purchased for them. I too have cooperated in this work and have paid the sorrows and afflictions, which thou hast understood and which I wish thou shalt never allow to be blotted out from my inmost memory. The Almighty would indeed have been powerful enough to exalt his predestined in this world, to give them riches and favors beyond those of others, to make them strong as lions for reducing the rest of mankind to their invincible power. But it was inopportune to exalt them in this manner, in order that men might not be led into the error of thinking that greatness consists in what is visible and happiness in earthly goods; lest, being induced to forsake virtues and obscure the glory of the Lord, they fail to experience the efficacy of divine grace and cease to aspire toward spiritual and eternal things. This is the science which I wish thee to study continually and in which thou must advance day by day, putting into practice all that thou learnest to understand and know.

Pilate Pronounces The Sentence of Death

Against the Author of Life; the Lord Takes Up the Cross On Which He Is To Die; His Most Holy Mother Follows Him; What She Did On This Occasion to Restraint the Devil, and Other Happenings

To the great satisfaction and joy of the priests and pharisees Pilate then decreed the sentence of death on the Cross against Life itself, Jesus our Savior. Having announced it to the One they had thus condemned in spite of his innocence, they brought Him to another part of the house of Pilate, where they stripped Him of the purple mantle, in which they had derided Him as mockking. All happened by the mysterious dispensation of God; though on their part it was due to the concerted malice of the Jews; for they wished to see Him undergo the punishment of the Cross in his own clothes so that in them He might be recognized by all. Only by his garments could He now be recognized by the people, since his face had been disfigured beyond recognition by the scourging, the impure spittle, and the crown of thorns. They again clothed Him with the seamless tunic, which at the command of the Queen was brought to Him by the angels; for the executioners had thrown it into a corner of another room in the house, where they left it to place upon Him the mocking and scandalous purple cloak. But the Jews neither understood nor noticed any of these circumstances, since they were too much taken up with the desire of hastening his Death.

Through the diligence of the Jews in spreading the news of the sentence decreed against Jesus of Nazareth, the people hastened in multitudes to the house of Pilate in order to see Him brought forth to execution. Since the ordinary number of inhabitants was increased by the gathering of numerous strangers from different parts to celebrate the Pasch, the city was fun of people. An of them were stirred by the news and fiJled the streets up to the very palace of Pilate. It was a Friday, the day of the Parasceve, which in Greek signifies preparation, or getting ready; for on that day the Jews prepared themselves, or got ready, for the ensuing Sabbath, their greatest feast, on which no servile work was to be performed, not even such as cooking meals; all this had to be done on this Friday. In the sight of all these multitudes they brought forth our Savior in his own garments and with a countenance so disfigured by wounds, blood and spittle, that no one would have again recognized Him as the One they had seen or known before. At the command of his afflicted :Mother the holy angels had a few times wiped off some of the impure spittle; but his enemies had so persistently continued in their disgusting insults, that now He appeared altogether covered by their vile expectorations. At the sight of such a sorrowful spectacle a confused shouting and clamor arose from the people, so that nothing could be understood, but an fonned one uproar and confusion of voices. But above all the rest were heard the shouts of the priests and pharisees, who in their unrestrained joy imd exultation harangued the people to become quiet and clear the streets through which the divine Victim was to pass, in order that they might hear the sentence of death proclaimed against Him. The people were divided and confused in their opinions, according to the suggestions of their own hearts. At this spectacle were present different kinds of people, who had been benefited and succored by the miracles and the kindness of Jesus, and such as had heard and accepted his teachings and had become his followers and friends. These now showed their sympathy, some in bitter tears, others by asking what this Man had done to deserve such punishment; others were dumbfounded and began to be troubled and confused by this universal confusion and tumult.

Of the eleven Apostles saint John alone was present. He with the sorrowful Mother and the three Marys stood within sight of the Lord, though in a retired corner. When the holy Apostle saw his divine Master brought forth, the thought of whose love toward himself now shot through his mind, he was so filled with grief, that his blood congealed in his veins and his face took on the appearance of death. The three Marys fell away into a prolonged swoon. But the Queen of virtues remained unconquered and her magnanimous heart, though overwhelmed by a grief beyond all conception of man, never fainted or swooned; She did not share the imperfections or weaknesses of the others. In all her actions She was most prudent, courageous and admirable; calmly She comforted saint John and the pious women. She besought the Lord to strengthen them, in order that She might have their company to the end of the Passion. In virtue of this prayer the Apostle and the holy women were consoled and encouraged, so that they regained their senses and could speak to the Mistress of heaven. Amid all this bitterness and confusion She did nothing unbecoming or inconsiderate, but shed forth incessant tears with the dignity of a Queen. Her attention was riveted upon Her Son, the true God; She prayed to the eternal Father and offered to Him his sorrows and torments, imitating in her actions all that was done by our Savior. She recognized the malice of sin, penetrated the mysteries of the

Redemption, appealed to the angels and interceded for friends and enemies. While giving way to her maternal love and to the sorrows corresponding to it, She at the same time practiced all the virtues, exciting the highest admiration of all heaven and delighting in the highest degree the eternal Godhead. Since it is not possible for me to describe the sentiments filling the heart of this Mother of wisdom, nor those at times also uttered by her lips, I leave them to be imagined by Christian piety.

The servants and priests sought to quiet the multitudes, in order that they might be able to hear the sentence pronounced against Jesus of Nazareth; for after it had been made known to Him in person, they desired to have it read before the people and in his presence. When the people had quieted down, they began to read it in a loud voice, so that all could hear it, while Jesus was standing in full view as a criminal. The sentence was proclaimed also in the different streets and at the foot of the Cross; and it was afterwards published and spread in many copies. According to the understanding given to me, the copies were a faithful reproduction, excepting some words which have been added. I will not discuss them, for the exact words of this sentence have been shown me and I give them here without change.

Literal Rendering of the Sentence of Death

Pronounces Against Jesus of Nazareth, Our Saviour

"I Pontius Pilate, presiding over lower Galilee and governing Jerusalem, in fealty to the Roman Empire, and being within the executive mansion, judge, decide, and proclaim, that I condemn to death, Jesus, of the Nazarean people and a Galileean by birth, a man seditious and opposed to our laws, to our senate, and to the great emperor Tiberius Cesar. For the execution of this sentence I decree, that his death be upon the cross and that He shall be fastened thereto with nails as is customary with criminals; because, in this very place, gathering around Him every day many men, poor and rich, He has continued to raise tumults throughout Judea, proclaiming Himself the Son of God and King of Israel, at the same time threatening the ruin of this renowned city of Jerusalem and its temple, and of the sacred Empire, refusing tribute to Cesar; and because He dared to enter in triumph this city of Jerusalem and the temple of Solomon, accompanied by a great multitude of the people carrying branches of palms. I command the first centurion, called Quintus Cornelius, to lead

Him for his greater shame through the said city of Jerusalem, bound as He is, and scourged by my orders. Let Him also wear his own garments, that He may be known to all, and let Him carry the Cross on which He is to be crucified. Let Him walk through all the public streets between two other thieves, who are likewise condemned to death for their robberies and murders, so that this punishment be an example to all the people and to all malefactors."

"I desire also and command in this my sentence, that this malefactor, having been thus led through the public streets, be brought outside the city through the pagora gate, now called the Antonian portal, and under the proclamations of the herald, who shall mention all the crimes pointed out in my sentence, He shall be conducted to the summit of the mountain called Calvary, where justice is wont to be executed upon wicked transgressors. There, fastened and crucified upon the Cross, which He shall carry as decreed above, his body shall remain between the aforesaid thieves. Above the Cross, that is, at its top, He shall have placed for Him his name and title in the three languages; namely in Hebrew, Greek and Latin; and in all and each one of them shall be written: THIS IS JESUS OF NAZARETH, KING OF THE JEWS, so that it may be understood by all and become universally known."

"At the same time I command, that no one, no matter of what condition, under pain of the loss of his goods and life, and under punishment for rebellion against the Roman empire, presume audaciously to impede the execution of this just sentence ordered by me to be executed with all rigor according to the decrees and laws of the Romans and Hebrews. Year of the creation of the world 5233, the twentyfifth day of March." Pontius Pilatus Judex et Gubernator Galilaeae inferioris pro Romano Imperio qui supra propria manu. (Pontius Pilate, Judge and Governor of lower Galilee for the Roman Empire, who signed the above with his own hand.)

According to the above reckoning the creation of the world happened in March; and from the day on which Adam was created until the Incarnation of the Word 5199 years; adding the nine months, during which He remained in the virginal womb of his most holy Mother, and the thirtythree years of his life, we complete the 5233 years and three months, which according to the reckoning of the Romans intervened between the anniversary of his birth and the 25th of March, the day of his death. According to the reckoning of the Roman Church there are not more than nine months and seven days to the first year, since it begins its count of years with the first of January of the second year of the world. Of all the opinions of the teachers of the Church I have understood the one which corresponds to the reckoning of the Roman Church in the Roman martyrology to be the correct one. This I have also stated in the chapter of the Incarnation of Christ our Lord in the first book of the second part, chapter eleventh.

The sentence of Pilate against our Savior having been published in a loud voice before all the people, the executioners loaded the heavy Cross, on which He was to be crucified, upon his tender and wounded shoulders. In order that He might carry it they loosened the bonds holding his hands, but not the others, since they wished to drag Him along by the loose ends of the ropes that bound his body. In order to torment Him the more they drew two loops around his throat. The Cross was fifteen feet long, of thick and heavy timbers. The herald began to proclaim the sentence and the whole confused and turbulent multitude of the people, the executioners and soldiers, with great noise, uproar and disorder began to move from the house of Pilate to mount Calvary through the streets of Jerusalem. The Master and Redeemer of the world, Jesus, before receiving the Cross, looked upon it with a countenance full of extreme joy and exultation such as would be shown by a bridegroom looking at the rich adornments of his bride, and on receiving it, He addressed it as follows:

"O Cross, beloved of my soul, now prepared and ready to still my longings, come to Me, that I may be received in thy arms, and that, attached to them as on an altar, I may be accepted by the eternal Father as the sacrifice of his everlasting reconciliation with the human race. In order to die upon thee, I have descended from heaven and assumed mortal and passible flesh; for thou art to be the sceptre with which I shall triumph over all my enemies, the key with which I shall open the gates of heaven for all the predestined (Isaias 22, 22), the sanctuary in which the guilty sons of Adam shall find mercy, and the treasure house for the enrichment of their poverty. Upon thee I desire to exalt and recommend dishonor and reproach among men, in order that my friends may embrace them with joy, seek them with anxious longings, and follow Me on the path which I through thee shall open up before them. My Father and eternal God, I confess Thee as the Lord of heaven and earth (Matthew 11, 25), subjecting Myself to thy power and to thy divine wishes, I take upon my shoulders the wood for the sacrifice of my innocent and passible humanity and I accept it willingly for the salvation of men. Receive Thou, eternal Father, this sacrifice as acceptable to thy justice, in order that from today on they may not any more be servants, but sons and heirs of thy kingdom together with Me" (Romans 8, 17).

None of these sacred mysteries and happenings were hidden from the great Lady of the world, Mary; for She had a most intimate knowledge and understanding of them, far beyond that of all the angels. The events, which She could not see with the eyes of her body, She perceived by her intelligence and revealed science, which manifested to Her the interior operation of her most holy Son. By this divine light She recognized the infinite value of the wood of the Cross after once it had come in contact with the deified humanity of Jesus our Redeemer. Immediately She venerated and adored it in a manner befitting it. The same was also done by the heavenly spirits attending upon the Queen. She imitated her divine Son in the tokens of affections, with which He received the Cross, addressing it in the words suited to her office as Coadjutrix of the Redeemer. By her prayers to the eternal Father She followed Him in his exalted sentiments as the living original and exemplar, without failing in the least point. When She heard the voice of the herald publishing and rehearsing the sentence through the streets, the heavenly Mother, in protest against the accusations contained in the sentence and in the form of comments on the glory and honor of the Lord, composed a canticle of praise and worship of the innocence and sinless ness of her allholy Son and God. In the composing of this canticle the holy angels helped Her, conjointly with them She arranged and repeated it, while the inhabitants of Jerusalem were blaspheming their own Creator and Savior.

As all the faith, knowledge and love of creatures, during this time of the Passion, was enshrined in its highest essence in the magnanimous soul of the Mother of wisdom, She alone had the most proper conception and correct judgment of the suffering and Death of God for men. Without for a moment failing in the attention necessary to exterior actions, her wisdom penetrated all the mysteries of the Redemption and the manner in which it was to be accomplished through the ignorance of the very men who were to be redeemed. She entered into the deepest consideration of the dignity of the One, who was suffering, of what He was suffering, from and for whom He was suffering. Of the dignity of the person of Christ our Redeemer, uniting within Himself the divine and the human natures, of their perfections and attributes, the most blessed Mary alone possessed the highest and intuitive knowledge outside of the Lord himself. On this account She alone among all mere creatures attached sufficient importance to the

Passion and Death of her Son and of the true God. Of what He suffered, She was not only an eyewitness, but She experienced it personally within Herself, occasioning the holy envy not only of men, but of the angels themselves. who were not thus favored. But they well knew that their great Queen and Mistress felt and suffered in soul and body the same torments and sorrows as her most holy Son and that the holy Trinity was inexpressibly pleased with Her; and therefore they sought to make up by their praise and worship for the pains which they could not share. Sometimes, when the sorrowful Mother could not personally witness the sufferings of her Son, She was made to feel in her virginal body and in her spirit the effects of his torments before her intelligence made Her aware of them. Thus surprised She would say: "Ah! what new martyrdom have they devised for my sweetest Lord and Master?" And then She would receive the clearest knowledge of what the Lord was enduring. The most loving Mother was so admirably faithful in her sufferings and in imitating the example of Christ our God, that She never permitted Herself any easement either of her bodily pains, such as rest, or nourishment, or sleep; nor any relaxation of the spirit, such as any consoling thoughts or considerations, except when She was visited from on high by divine influence. Then only would She humbly and thankfully accept relief, in order that She might recover strength to attend still more fervently to the object of her sorrows and to the cause of his sufferings. The same wise consideration She applied to the malicious behavior of the Jews and their servants, to the needs of the human race, to their threatening ruin, and to the ingratitude of men, for whom He suffered. Thus She perfectly and intimately knew of all these things and felt it more deeply than all the creatures.

Another hidden and astonishing miracle was wrought by the right hand of God through the instrumentality of the blessed Mary against Lucifer and his infernal spirits. It took place in the following manner: The dragon and his associates, though they could not understand the humiliation of the Lord, were most attentive to all that happened in the Passion of the Lord. Now, when He took upon Himself the Cross, all these enemies felt a new and mysterious tremor and weakness, which caused in them great consternation and confused distress. Conscious of these unwonted and invincible feelings the prince of darkness feared, that in the Passion and Death of Christ our Lord some dire and irreparable destruction of his reign was imminent. In order not to be overtaken by it in the presence of Christ our God, the dragon resolved to retire and fly with all his followers to the caverns of hell. But when he sought to execute this resolve, he was prevented by the great Queen and Mistress of all creation; for the Most High, enlightening Her and intimating to Her what She was to do, at the same time invested Her with his power. The heavenly Mother, turning toward Lucifer and his squadrons, by her imperial command hindered them from flying; ordering them to await and witness the Passion to the end on mount Calvary. The demons could not resist the command of the mighty Queen; for they recognized and felt the divine power operating in Her. Subject to her sway they followed Christ as so many prisoners dragged along in chains to Calvary, where the eternal wisdom had decreed to triumph over them from the throne of the Cross, as we shall see later on. There is nothing which can exemplify the discouragement and dismay, which from that moment began to oppress Lucifer and his demons. According to our way of speaking, they walked along to Calvary like criminals condemned to a terrible death, and seized by the dismay and consternation of an inevitable punishment. This punishment of the demon was in conformity with his malicious nature and proportioned to the evil committed by him in introducing death and sin into the world, to remedy which, God himself was now undergoing Death.

Our Savior proceeded on the way to Calvary bearing upon his shoulders, according to the saying of Isaias, his own government and principality (Isaias 9, 6), which was none else than his Cross, from whence He was to subject and govern the world, meriting thereby that his name should be exalted above all other names and rescuing the human race from the tyrannical power of the demon over the sons of Adam (Colossians 2, 15). The same Isaias calls it the yoke and sceptre of the oppressor and executor, who was imperiously exacting the tribute of the first guilt. In order to destroy this tyrant and break the sceptre of his reign and the yoke of our servitude, Christ our Savior placed the Cross upon his shoulders; namely, upon that place, where are borne both the yoke of slavery and the sceptre of royal power. He wished to intimate thereby, that He despoiled the demon of this power and transferred it to his own shoulders, in order that thenceforward the captive children of Adam should recognize Him for their legitimate Lord and true King. All mortals were to follow Him in the way of the Cross (Matthew 14, 24) and learn, that by this Cross they were subjected to his power (John 12, 32) and now become his vassals and servants, bought by his own lifeblood (I Corinthians 4, 20).

But alas, the pity of our most ungrateful forgetfulness! That the Jews and ministers of the Passion should be ignorant of this mystery hidden to princes of this world, and that they should not dare touch the Cross of the Savior, because they considered it the wood of ignominy and shame, was their own fault and a very great one. Yet not so great as our own, since its mystery being already revealed to us, we spend our indignation only on the blindness of those who were persecuting our Lord and God. For, if we blame them for being ignorant of what they ought to have known, how much should we blame ourselves, who, knowing and confessing Christ the Redeemer, persecute and crucify Him by our offenses (Hebrews 6, 6)? O my sweetest Love, Jesus, light of my intellect and glory of my soul! Do not, O my Lord, trust in my sluggish torpidity to follow Thee with my Cross on thy way! Take it upon Thee to do me this favor; draw me after Thee, to run after the fragrance of thy sweetest love (Canticles 1, 3) of thy ineffable patience, of thy deepest humility, that I may desire for contempt and anguish, and seek after participation in thy ignominy, insults and sorrows. Let this be my portion and my inheritance in this mortal and oppressing life, let this be my glory and my repose; and outside of the Cross and its ignominy, I desire not to live or be consoled or to partake of any rest or enjoyment. As the Jews and all of that blind multitude avoided the touch of the Cross of Him, who was so innocently sentenced to die upon it, He opened with it a passage and cleared for Himself a way. His perfidious persecutors looked upon his glorious dishonor as a contagion and they fled from its approach, though all the rest of the streets were full of shouting and clamoring people, who crowded aside as the herald advanced proclaiming the sentence.

The executioners, bare of all human compassion and kindness, dragged our Savior Jesus along with incredible cruelty and insults. Some of them jerked Him forward by the ropes in order to accelerate his passage, while others puuled from behind in order to retard it. On account of this jerking and the weight of the Cross they caused Him to sway to and fro and often to faU to the ground. By the hard knocks He thus received on the rough stones great wounds were opened, especially on the two knees and they were widened at each repeated fall. The heavy Cross also inflicted a wound on the shoulder on which it was carried. The unsteadiness caused the Cross sometimes to knock against his sacred head, and sometimes the head against the Cross; thus the thorns of his crown penetrated deeper and wounded the parts, which they had not yet reached. To these torments of the body the ministers of evil added many insulting words and execrable affronts, ejecting their impure spittle and throwing the dirt of the pavement into his face so mercilessly, that they blinded the eyes that looked upon them with such divine mercy. Thus they of their own account condemned themselves to the loss of the graces, with which his very looks were fraught. By the haste with which they dragged Him along in their eagerness to see Him die, they did not allow Him to catch his breath; for his most innocent body, having been in so few hours overwhelmed with such a storm of torments, was so weakened and bruised, that to all appearances He was ready to yield up life under his pains and sorrows.

From the house of Pilate the sorrowful and stricken Mother followed with the multitudes on the way of her divine Son, accompanied by saint John and the pious women. As the surging crowds hindered Her from getting very near to the Lord, She asked the eternal Father to be permitted to stand at the foot of the Cross of her blessed Son and see Him die with her own eyes. With the divine consent She ordered her holy angels to manage things in such a way as to make it possible for Her to execute her wishes. The holy angels obeyed Her with great reverence; and they speedily led the Queen through some bystreet, in order that She might meet her Son. Thus it came that both of Them met face to face in sweetest recognition of each Other and in mutual renewal of each other's interior sorrows. Yet They did not speak to one another, nor would the fierce cruelty of the executioners have permitted such an intercourse. But the 1110st prudent Mother adored her divine Son and true God, laden with the Cross; and interiorly besought Him, that, since She could not relieve Him of the weight of the Cross and since She was not permitted to command her holy angels to lighten it, He would inspire these ministers of cruelty to procure some one for his assistance. This prayer was heard by the Lord Christ; and so it happened, that Simon of Cyrene was afterwards impressed to carry the Cross with the Lord (Matthew 27,32). The pharisees and the executioners were moved to this measure, some of them out of natural compassion, others for fear lest Christ, the Author of life, should lose his life by exhaustion before it could be taken from Him on the Cross.

Beyond all human thought and estimation was the sorrow of the most sincere Dove and Virgin 1Iother while She thus witnessed with her own eyes her Son carrying the Cross to Mount Calvary; for She alone could fittingly know and love Him according to his true worth. It would have been impossible for Her to live through this ordeal, if the divine power had not strengthened Her and preserved Her life. With bitterest sorrow She addressed the Lord and spoke to Him in her heart: "My Son and eternal God, light of my eyes and life of my soul, receive, O Lord, the sacrifice of my not being able to relieve Thee of the burden of the Cross and carry it myself, who am a daughter of Adam; for it is I who should die upon it in love of Thee, as Thou now wishest to die in most ardent love of the human race. O most loving Mediator between guilt and justice! How dost Thou cherish mercy in the midst of so great injuries and such heinous offenses! O charity without measure or bounds, which permits such torments and affronts in order to afford it a wider scope for its ardor and efficacy! O infinite and sweetest love, would that the hearts and the wills of men were all mine, so that they could give no such thankless return for all that Thou endurest! O who will speak to the hearts of the mortals to teach them what they owe to Thee, since Thou hast paid so dearly for their salvation from ruin!" Other most prudent and exalted sentiments besides these were conceived by the great Lady, so that I cannot express them by words of mine.

As the Evangelist tells us, there were other women among the crowds, who followed the Savior bitter tears and lamentations (Luke 23, 27). The sweetest Jesus turning toward them, addressed them a said: "Daughters of Jerusalem, weep not over Me; but weep for yourselves and for your children. For behold the days shall come, wherein they shall say: Blesssed are the barren, and the wombs that have not born and the paps that have not given suck. Then shall they begin to say to the mountains: Fall upon us, and the hills: Cover us. For if in the green wood they these things, what shall be done in the dry?" By the mysterious words the Lord acknowledged the tears shed on account of his Passion, and to a certain extent, showing his appreciation of them, He approved of the in these women He wished to teach us for what purpose our tears should be shed so that they may attain their end. These compassionate disciples of the Lord we at that time ignorant of the true reason for their tea since they wept over his sufferings and injuries, a not over the cause of these sufferings; and therefore they merited to be instructed and admonished of the truth. It was as if the Savior had said to them: Weep over your sins and over the sins of your children, a attribute what I suffer to those sins. I suffer not for my sins, for I am guilty of none and it is not even possible that I be guilty of any. If I approve of your compassion for Me as good and just, much more do desire you to weep over your sins, for which I suffer and by this manner of weeping you shall acquire yourselves and your children the price of my blood and of my Redemption, ignored by this blind people. If there shall come days, namely the days of universal judgment and chastisement, in which those shall be held fortunate, who have not begotten children; and the fore-known shall call upon the mountains and the hills to shield them against my wrath. For if their sins, now only assumed by Me, have such effects on me, who am innocent, what horrible punishments will they draw upon those, who are so barren and without any fruits of grace and merits?

As a reward for their tears and their compassion these women were enlightened so as tei understand this doctrine. In fulfillment of the prayerful wish of the blessed Mother the pharisees and ministers were inspired with the resolve to engage some man to help Jesus our Savior in carrying the Cross to mount Calvary. At this juncture, Simon, of Cyrene, the father of the disciples Alexander and Rufus (Mark 15, 21), happened to come along. He was called by this name because he was a native of Cyrene, a city of Lybia, and had come to Jerusalem. This Simon was now forced by the Jews to carry the Cross a part of the way. They themselves would not touch it, yea would not even come near it, as being the instrument of punishment for One whom they held to be a notorious malefactor. By this pretended caution and avoidance of his Cross they sought to impress the people with a horror for Jesus. The Cyrenean took hold of the Cross and Jesus was made to follow between the two thieves, in order that all might believe Him to be a criminal and malefactor like to them. The Virgin Mother walked very closely behind Jesus, as She had desired and asked from the eternal Father. To his divine will She so conformed Herself in all the labors and torments of her Son that, witnessing with her own eyes and partaking of all the sufferings of her Son in her blessed soul and in her body, She never allowed any sentiment or wish to arise interiorly or exteriorly, which could be interpreted as regret for the sacrifice She had made in offering her Son for the death of the Cross and its sufferings. Her charity and love of men, and her grace and holiness, were so great, that She vanquished all these movements of her human nature.

Instruction, which Mary, the Queen of Heaven Gave Me

I desire that the fruit of the obedience with which thou writest the history of my life shall be, that thou become a true disciple of my most holy Son and of myself. The main purpose of the exalted and venerable mysteries, which are made known to thee, and of the teachings, which I so often repeat to thee, is that thou deny and strip thyself, estranging thy heart from all affection to creatures, neither wishing to possess them nor accept them for other uses. By this precaution thou wilt overcome the impediments, which the devils seek to place in the way of the dangerous softness of thy nature. I who know thee, thus advise and lead thee by the way of instruction and correction as thy Mother and Instructress. By the divine teaching thou knowest the mysteries of the Passion and Death of Christ and the one true way of life, which is the Cross; and thou knowest that not all who are called, are chosen. Many there are who wish to follow Christ and very few who truly dispose themselves to imitate Him; for as soon as they feel the sufferings of the Cross they cast it aside. Laborious exertions are very painful and averse to human nature according to the flesh; and the fruits of the spirit are more hidden and few guide themselves by the light. On this account there are so many among mortals, who, forgetful of the eternal truths, seek the flesh and the continual indulgence of its pleasures. They ardently seek honors and fly from injuries: they strive after riches, and contemn poverty; they long after pleasure and dread mortification. All these are enemies of the Cross of Christ (Philippians 3, 18), and with dread ful aversion they fly from it, deeming it sheer ignominy, just like those who crucified Christ, the Lord.

Another deceit has spread through the world: many imagine that they are following Christ their Master, though they neither suffer affliction nor engage in any exertion or labor. They are content with avoiding boldness in committing sins, and place all their perfection in a certain prudence or hollow selflove, which prevents them from denying anything to their will and from practicing any virtues at the cost of their flesh. They would easily escape this deception, if they would consider that my Son was not only the Redeemer, but their Teacher; and that He left in this world the treasures of his Redemption not only as a remedy against its eternal ruin, but as a necessary medicine for the sickness of sin in human nature. No one knew so much as my Son and Lord; no one could better understand the quality of love than the divine Lord, who was and is wisdom and charity itself; and no one was more able to fulfill all his wishes (I John 4, 16). Nevertheless, although He well could do it, He chose not a life of softness and ease for the flesh, but one full of labors and pains; for He judged his instructions to be incomplete and insufficient to redeem man, if He failed to teach them how to overcome the demon, the flesh and their own self. He wished to inculcate, that this magnificent victory is gained by the Cross, by labors, penances, mortifications and the acceptance of contempt: all of which are the trademarks and evidences of true love and the special watchwords of the predestined.

Thou, my daughter, knowest the value of the holy Cross and the honor which it confers upon ignominies and tribulations; do thou embrace the Cross and bear it with joy in imitation of my Son and thy Master (Matthew 16, 24). In this mortal life let thy glory be in tribulations, persecutions (Romans 5, 3), contempt, infirmities, poverty, humiliation and in whatever is painful and averse to mortal flesh. And in order that in all thy exercises thou mayest imitate me and give me pleasure, I wish that thou seek no rest or consolation in any earthly thing. Thou must not dwell in thy thoughts upon what thou bearest, nor seek to relieve thyself by enlisting the compassion of others. Much less must thou make much of, or try to impress others with the recital of the persecutions or molestations of creatures, nor should it ever be heard from thy lips, how much thou endurest, nor shouldst thou compare thy sufferings with those of others. I do not wish to say, that it is a sin to accept of some reasonable and moderate alleviation, or to mention thy afflictions. But in thee, my dearest, much alleviation, if not a sin, would be an infidelity to thy Spouse and Lord; for He has put thee personally under more obligation than many generations of men and thy response in suffering and love will be defective. and wanting, if it is not complete and loyal in all respects. So faithful does the Lord wish thy correspondence to be, that thou must allow thy weak nature not even one sigh for mere natural relief and consolation. If love alone impels thee, thou wilt allow thyself to be carried along by its sweet force and rest in it alone; and the love of the Cross would immediately dispense with such natural relief, in the same way as thou knowest I have done in my total self-sacrifice. Let this be to thee a general rule: that all human consolation is an imperfection and a danger, and that thou shouldst welcome only that, which the Most High sends to thee Himself or through his holy angels. And even these favors of the divine right hand thou must accept only in so far as they strengthen thee to suffer more constantly and to withdraw thee from all that ministers to the senses.

How Our Savior Jesus Was Crucified on Mount Calvary

The Seven Word Spoken By Him On the Cross and the Attendance of His Sorrowful Mother At His Sufferings

Our Savior then, the new and true Isaac, the Son of the eternal Father, reached the mountain of sacrifice, which is the same one to which his prototype and figure, Isaac, was brought by the patriarch Abraham (Genesis 22, 9). Upon the most innocent Lamb of God was to be executed the rigor of the sentence, which had been suspended in favor of the son of the Patriarch. Mount Calvary was held to be a place of defilement and ignominy, as being reserved for the chastisement of condemned criminals, whose cadavers spread around it their stench and attached to it a still more evil fame. Our most loving Jesus arrived at its summit so worn out, wounded, torn and disfigured, that He seemed altogether transformed into an object of pain and sorrows. The power of the Divinity, which deified his most holy humanity by its hypostatical union, helped Him, not to lighten his pains, but to strengthen Him against death; so that, still retaining life until death should be permitted to take it away on the Cross, He might satiate his love to the fullest extent. The sorrowful and afflicted Mother, in the bitterness of her soul, also arrived at the summit of the mount and remained very close to her divine Son; but in the sorrows of her soul She was as it were beside Herself, being entirely transformed by her love and by the pains which She saw Jesus suffer. Near her were saint John and the three Marys; for they alone, through her intercession and the favor of the eternal Father, had obtained the privilege of remaining so constantly near to the Savior and to his Cross.

When the most prudent Mother perceived that now the mysteries of the Redemption were to be fulfilled and that the executioners were about to strip Jesus of his clothes for crucifixion, She turned in spirit to the eternal Father and prayed as follows: "My Lord and eternal God, Thou art the l'ather of thy Only-begotten Son. By eternal generation He is engendered, God of the true God, namely Thyself, and as man He was born of my womb and received from me this human nature, in which He now suffers. I have nursed and sustained Him at my own breast; and as the best of sons that ever can be born of any creature, I love Him with maternal love. As his Mother I have a natural right in the Person of his most holy humanity and thy Providence will never infringe upon any rights held by thy creatures.

This right of a Mother then, I now yield to Thee and once more place in thy hands thy and my Son as a sacrifice for the H.edemption of man. Accept, my Lord, this pleasing offering, since this is more than I can ever offer by submitting my own self as a victim or to suffering. This sacrifice is greater, not only because my Son is the true God and of thy own substance, but because this sacrifice costs me a much greater sorrow and pain. For if the lots were changed and I should be permitted to die in order to preserve his most holy life, I would consider it a great relief and the fulfillment of my dearest wishes." The eternal Father received this prayer of the exalted Queen with ineffable pleasure and complacency. The patriarch Abraham was permitted to go no further than to prefigure and attempt the sacrifice of a son, because the real execution of such a sacrifice God reserved to Himself and to his Only-begotten. Nor was Sara, the mother of Isaac, in formed of the mystical ceremony, this being prevented not only by the promptness of Abraham's obedience, but also because he mistrusted, lest the maternal love of Sara, though she was a just and holy woman, should impel her to prevent the execution of the divine command. But not so was it with most holy Mary, to whom the eternal Father could fearlessly manifest his unchangeable will in order that She might, as far as her powers were concerned, unite with Him in the sacrifice of his Only-begotten.

The invincible Mother finished her prayer and She perceived that the impious ministers were preparing to give to the Lord the drink of wine, myrrh and gall, of which saint Matthew and saint Mark speak (Matthew 27, 34; Mark 15. 23). Taking occasion from the words of Solomon: Give strong drink to the sorrowful and wine to those that suffer bitterness of heart, the Jews were accustomed to give to those about to be executed a drink of strong and aromatic wine in order to raise their vital spirits and to help them to bear their torments with greater fortitude. This custom they now perverted in order to augment the sufferings of the Savior (Proverbs 3,6). The drink, which was intended to assist and strengthen other criminals, by the perfidy of the Jews was now mixed with gall, so that it should have no other effect than to torment his sense of taste by its bitterness. The blessed Mother was aware of their intentions and in her maternal tenderness and compassion asked the Lord not to drink of it. Jesus in deference to the petition of his Mother, without rejecting entirely this new suffering, tasted of the mixture, but would not drink it entirely (Matthew 27, 34).

It was already the sixth hour, which corresponds to our noontime, and the executioners, intending to crucify the Savior naked, despoiled Him of the seamless tunic and of his garments. As the tunic was large and without opening in front, they pulled it over the head of Jesus without taking off the crown of thorns; but on account of the rudeness with which they proceeded, they inhumanly tore off the crown with the tunic. Thus they opened anew all the wounds of his head, and in some of them remained the thorns, which, in spite of their being so hard and sharp, were wrenched off by the violence with which the executioners despoiled Him of his tunic and, with it, of the crown. With heartless cruelty they again forced it down upon his sacred head, opening up wounds upon wounds. By the rude tearing off of the tunic were renewed also the wounds of his whole body, since the tunic had dried into the open places and its removal was, as David says, adding new pains to his wounds (Psalms 68, 27). Four times during the Passion did they despoil Jesus of his garments and again vest Him. The first time in order to scourge Him at the pillar; the second time in order to clothe Him in the mock purple; the third, when they took this off in order to clothe Him in his tunic; the fourth, when they finally took away his clothes. This last was the most painful, because his wounds were more numerous, his holy humanity was much weakened, and there was less shelter against the sharp wind on mount Calvary; for also this element was permitted to increase the sufferings of his deathstruggle i>y sending its cold blasts across the mount. To all these sufferings was added the confusion of being bereft of his garments in the presence of his most blessed Mother, of her pious companions, and in full sight of the multitudes gathered around. By his divine power He, however, reserved for Himself the nether garment which his Mother had wound around his loins in Egypt; for neither at the scourging, nor at the crucifixion could the executioners remove it, and He was laid in the sepulchre still covered with this cloth. That this really happened, has been revealed to me many times. Certainly, He desired to die in the greatest poverty and to take with Him nothing of all that He created and possessed in this world. He would gladly have died entirely despoiled and bereft of even this covering, if it had not been for the desires and the prayers of his blessed Mother, to which Christ wished to yield. On her account He substituted this most perfect obedience of a Son toward his Mother for extreme poverty at his Death. The holy Cross was lying on the ground and the executioners were busy making the necessary preparations for crucifying Him and the two thieves. In the meanwhile our Redeemer and Master prayed to the Father in the following terms:

"Eternal Father and my Lord God, to the incomprehensible Majesty of thy infinite goodness and justice I offer my entire humanity and all that according to thy will it has accomplished in descending from thy bosom to assume passible and mortal flesh for the Redemption of men, my breLamentations I offer Thee, Lord, with Myself, also my most loving Mother, her love, her most perfect works, her sorrows, her sufferings, her anxious and prudent solicitude in serving Me, imitating Me and accompanying Me unto death. I offer Thee the little flock of my Apostles, the holy Church and congregation of the faithful, such as it is now and as it shall be to the end of the world; and with it I offer to Thee all the mortal children of Adam. All this I place in thy hands as the true and almighty Lord and God. As far as my wishes are concerned, I suffer and die for all, and I desire that all shall be saved, under the condition that all follow Me and profit of my Redemption. Thus may they pass from the slavery of the devil to be thy children, my brethren and coheirs of the grace merited by Me. Especially, O my Lord, do I offer to Thee the poor, the despised and afflicted, who are my friends and who follow Me on the way to the Cross. I desire that the just and the predestined be written in thy eternal memory. I beseech Thee, my Father, to withhold thy chastisement and not to raise the scourge of thy justice over men; let them not be punished as they merit for their sins. Be Thou from now on their Father as Thou art mine. I beseech Thee also, that they may be helped to ponder upon my Death in pious affection and be enlightened from above; and I pray for those who are persecuting Me, in order that they may be converted to the truth. Above all do I ask Thee for the exaltation of thy ineffable and most holy name."

This prayer and supplication of our Savior Jesus were known to the most blessed Mother, and She imitated Him and made the same petitions to the eternal Father in as far as She was concerned. The most prudent Virgin never forgot or disregarded the first word which She had heard from the mouth of her divine Son as an infant: "Become like unto Me, my Beloved." His promise, that in return for the new human existence which She had given Him in her virginal womb, He would, by his almighty power, give Her a new existence of divine and eminent grace above all other creatures, was continually fulfilled. To this favor was due also her deep science and enlightenment concerning all the operations of the sacred humanity of her Son, none of which ever escaped her knowledge and attention. Whatever She thus perceived She imitated; so that She was always anxious to study and penetrate them with deep understanding, to put them promptly into action, and to practice them courageously and zealously during all her life. In this neither sorrow could disturb Her, nor anguish hinder Her, nor persecution detain Her, nor the bitterness of her suffering weaken Her. If the great Queen had assisted at the Passion with the same sentiments as the rest of the just, it would indeed have been admirable; but not so admirable as the way in which She suffered. She was singular and extraordinary in all her sufferings; for, as I have said above, She felt in her own virginal body all the torments of Christ our Lord, both interior and exterior. On account of this conformity we can say, that also the heavenly Mother was scourged. crowned, spit upon, buffeted, laden with the Cross and nailed upon it; for She felt these pains and all the rest in her purest body. Although She felt them in a different manner, yet She felt them with such conformity that the Mother was altogether a faithful likeness of her Son. Besides the greatness of her dignity, which in most holy Mary must, on this account, have corresponded in the highest possible degree with that of Christ, there was concealed therein another mystery. This was, that the desire of Christ to see his exalted love and benignity as exhibited in his Passion copied in all its magnitude in a mere creature, was fulfilled in Her, and no one possessed a greater right to this favor than his own Mother.

In order to find the places for the auger holes on the Cross, the executioners haughtily commanded the Creator of the universe. (O dreadful temerity!), to stretch Himself out upon it. The Teacher of humility obeyed without hesitation. But they, following their inhuman instinct of cruelty, marked the places for the holes, not according to the size of his body, but larger, having in mind a new torture for their VicTimothy This inhuman intent was known to the Mother of light, and the knowledge of it was one of the greatest afflictions of her chastest heart during the whole Passion. She saw through the intentions of these ministers of sin and She anticipated the torments to be endured by her beloved Son when his limbs should be wrenched from their sockets in being nailed to the Cross. But She could not do anything to prevent it, as it was the will of the Lord to suffer these pains for men. When He rose from the Cross, and they set about boring the holes, the great Lady approached and took hold of one of his hands, adoring Him and kissing it with greatest reverence. The executioners allowed this because they thought that the sight of his Mother would cause so much the greater affliction to the Lord; for they wished to spare Him no sorrow they could cause Him. But they were ignorant of the hidden mysteries; for the Lord during his Passion had no greater source of consolation and interior joy than to see in the soul of his most hlessed Mother, the beautiful likeness of Himself and the full fruits of his Passion and Death. This joy, to a certain extent, comforted Christ our Lord also in that hour.

Having bored the three holes into the Cross, the executioners again commanded Christ the Lord to stretch Himself out upon it in order to be nailed to it. The supreme and almighty King, as the Author of patience, obeyed, and at the will of the hangmen, placed Himself with outstretched arms upon the blessed wood. The Lord was so weakened, disfigured and exhausted. that if the ferocious cruelty of those men had left the least room for natural reason and kindness, they could not have brought themselves to inflict further torments upon the innocent and meek Lamb, humbly suffering such nameless sorrows and pains. But not so with them; for the judges and their executioners (O terrible and most hidden judgments of the Lord!) were transformed in their malice and deathly hatred into demons, void of the feelings of sensible and earthly men and urged on only by diabolical wrath and fury.

Presently one of the executioners seized the hand of Jesus our Savior and placed it upon the auger hole, while another hammered a large and rough nail through the palm. The veins and sinews were torn, and the bones of the sacred hand, which made the heavens and all that exists, were forced apart. When they stretched out the other hand, they found that it did not reach up to the augerhole; for the sinews of the other arm had been shortened and the executioners had maliciously set the holes too far apart, as I have mentioned above. In order to overcome the difficulty, they took the chain. with which the Savior had been bound in the garden, and looping one end through a ring around his wrist, they, with unheard of cruelty, pulled the hand over the hole and fastened it with another nail. Thereupon they seized his feet, and placing them one above the other, they tied the same chain around both and stretched them with barbarous ferocity down to the third hole. Then they drove through both feet a large nail into the Cross. Thus the sacred body, in which dwelled the Divinity, was nailed motionless to the holy Cross, and the handiwork of his deified members, formed by the Holy Ghost, was so stretched and tom asunder, that the bones of his body, dislocated and forced from their natural position, could all be counted. The bones of his breast, of his shoulders and arms, and of his whole body yielded to the cruel violence and were tom from their sinews.

It is impossible for human tongue or words of mouth to describe the torments of our Savior Jesus and what He suffered on this occasion. On the last day alone more will be known, in order that his cause may be justified before sinners and the praise and exaltation of the saints may be so much the greater. But at present, while our faith in this truth gives us occasion and obliges us to apply our reason (if such we possess), I ask, implore and beseech the children of the holy Church, each one for Himself, to study this most venerable sacrament. Let us contemplate it and weigh it with all its circumstances, and we shall find powerful motives to abhor and firmly resolve to avoid sin, as the cause of all this suffering to the Author of life. Let us contemplate and look upon his Virgin Mother, so afflicted in spirit and overwhelmed by the torments of her purest body, in order that through this gate of light we may enter to see the Sun that illumines our heart. O Mistress and Queen of virtues! O true Mother of the immortal King of ages become man! It is true, O my Lady, that the hardness of our ungrateful hearts makes us very unfit and unworthy of suffering thy pains and those of thy most holy Son our Lord; but through thy clemency make us partakers of this favor, which we do not deserve. Purify and free us from this deadening lukewarmness and gross neglect. If we are the cause of these sufferings, what propriety or what justice can there be in visiting them only on Thee and on thy Beloved? Let the chalice pass from the lips of the Innocent, in order that it may be tasted by the guilty who deserve it. But alas! Where is our good sense? Where wisdom and knowledge? Where is the light of our eyes? Who has so entirely deprived us of our understanding? Who has robbed us of our human and sensible hearts? If I, O Lord, had not received from Thee this being according to thy image and likeness; if Thou hadst not given me life and motion; if all the elements and creatures, formed by thy hand for my service (Ecclesiaticus 39, 30), were not giving me continual notice of thy immense love: at least thy being nailed so outrageously to the Cross, and all thy torments and sorrows for my salvation, should have sufficed to draw me to Thee with the bonds of compassion and gratitude, of love and confidence in thy ineffable kindness. But if so many voices cannot awaken me, if such love does not enkindle mine, if thy Passion and Death do not mm'e me, if such great benefits cannot oblige me, what end shall I expect as the result of my foolishness?

After the Savior was nailed to the Cross, the executioners judged it necessary to bend the points of the nails which projected through the back of the wood, in order that they might not be loosened and drawn out by the weight of the body. For this purpose they raised up the Cross in order to turn it over, so that the body of the Lord would rest face downward upon the ground with the weight of the Cross upon Him. This new cruelty appalled all the bystanders and a shout of pity arose in the crowd. But the sorrowful and compassionate Mother intervened by her prayers, and asked the eternal Father not to permit this boundless. outrage to happen in the way the executioners had intended. She commanded her holy angels to come to the assistance of their Creator. When, therefore, the executioners raised up the Cross to let it fall, with the crucified Lord face downward upon the ground, the holy angels supported Him and the Cross above the stony and fetid ground, so that his divine countenance did not come in contact with the rocks and pebbles. Thus altogether ignorant of the miracle the executioners bent over the points of the nails; for the sacred body was so near to the ground and the Cross was so firmly held by the angels, that the Jews thought it rested upon the hard rock.

Then they dragged the lower end of the Cross with the crucified God near to the hole, wherein it was to be planted. Some of them getting under the upper part of the Cross with their shoulders, others pushing upward with their halberds and lances, they raised the Savior on his Cross and fastened its foot in the hole they had drilled into the ground. Thus our true life and salvation now hung in the air upon the sacred wood in full view of the innumerable multitudes of different nations and countries. I must not omit mentioning another barbarity inflicted upon the Lord as they raised Him: for some of them placed the sharp points of their lances and halberds to his body and fearfully laceratingHim under the armpits in helping to push the Cross into position. At this spectacle new cries of protest arose with still more vehemence and confusion from the multitude of people. The Jews blasphemed, the kindhearted lamented, the strangers were astounded, some of them called the attention of the bystanders to the proceedings, others turned away their heads in horror and pity; others took to themselves a warning from this spectacle of suffering, and still others proclaimed Him a just Man. All these different sentiments were like arrows piercing the heart of the afflicted Mother. The sacred body now shed much blood from the nail wounds, which, by its weight and the shock of the Cross falling into the hole, had widened. They were the fountains, now opened up, to which Isaias invites us to hasten with joy to quench our thirst and wash off the stains of our sins (Isaias 12, 3). No one shall be excused who does not quickly approach to drink of them; since the waters are sold without exchange of silver or gold, and they are given freely to those who will but receive them (Isaias 54, 1).

Then they crucified also the two thieves and planted their crosses to the right and the left of the Savior; for thereby they wished to indicate that He deserved the most conspicuous place as being' the greatest malefactor. The pharisees and priests, forgetting the two thieves, turned all the venom of their fury against the sinless and holy One by nature. Wagging their heads in scorn and mockery (Matthew 27, 39) they threw stones and dirt at the Cross of the Lord and his royal Person, saying: "Ah Thou, who destroyest the temple and in three days rebuildest it, save now Thyself; others He has made whole, Himself He cannot save; if this be the Son of God let Him descend from the Cross, and we will believe in Him" (Matthew 27, 42). The two thieves in the beginning also mocked the Lord and said: "If Thou art the Son of God, save Thyself and us." These blasphemies of the two thieves caused special sorrow to our Lord, since they were so near to death and were losing the fruit of their death pains, by which they could have satisfied in part for their justly punished crimes. Soon after, however, one of them availed himself of the greatest opportunity that a sinner ever had in this world, and was converted from his sins.

When the great Queen of the angels, most holy Mary, perceived that the Jews in their perfidy and obstinate envy vied in dishonoring Him, in blaspheming Him as the most wicked of men and in desiring to blot out his name from the land of the living, as Jeremias had prophesied (Jeremias 11, 19), She was inflamed with a new zeal for the honor of her Son and true God. Prostrate before the person of the Crucified, and adoring Him, She besought the eternal Father to see to the honor of his Only-begotten and manifest it by such evident signs that the perfidy of the Jews might be confounded and their malice frustrated of its intent. Having presented this petition to the Father, She, with the zeal and authority of the Queen of the universe, addressed all the irrational creatures and said: "Insensible creatures, created by the hand of the Almighty, do you manifest your compassion, which in deadly foolishness is denied to Him by men capable of reason. Ye heavens, thou sun, moon and ye stars and planets, stop in your course and suspend your activity in regard to mortals. Ye elements, change your condition, earth lose thy stability, let your rocks and cliffs be rent. Ye sepulchres and monuments of the dead. open and send forth your contents for the confusion of the living. Thou mystical and figurative veil of the temple, divide into two parts and by thy separation threaten the unbelievers with chastisement, give witness to the truth and to the glory of their Creator and Redeemer, which they are trying to obscure."

In virtue of this prayer and of the commands of Mary, the Mother of the Crucified, the Omnipotence of God had provided for all that was to happen at the death of his Only-begotten. The Lord enlightened and moved the hearts of many of the bystanders at the time of these happenings on earth, and even before that time, in order that they might confess Jesus crucified as holy, just and as the true Son of God. This happened, for instance, with the centurion and many others mentioned in the Gospels, who went away from Calvary striking their breasts in sorrow. Among them were not only those who previously had heard and belined his doctrine, but also a great number of such as had never seen Him or witnessed his miracles. For the same reason Pilate was also inspired not to change the title of the Cross which they had placed over the head of the Savior in Hebrew, Greek and Latin. For when the Jews protested and asked Him not to write: Jesus of Nazareth, King of the Jews; but: This one says, He is King of the Jews; Pilate answered: What is written, is written, and I do not wish it to be changed. All the inanimate creatures, by divine will, obeyed the command of the most holy Mary. From the noon hour until three o'clock in the afternoon, which was called the ninth hour, when the Lord expired, they exhibited the great disturbances and changes mentioned in the Gospels. The sun hid its light, the planets showed great alterations, the earth quaked, many mountains were rent; the rocks shook one against the other, the graves opened and sent forth some of the dead alive. The changes in the elements and in the whole universe were so notable and extraordinary that they were evident on the whole earth. All the Jews of Jerusalem were dismayed and astonished; although their outrageous perfidy and malice made them unworthy of the truth and hindered them from accepting what all the insensible creatures preached to them.

The soldiers who had crucified Jesus our Savior, according to a custom permitting the executioners to take possession of the property of those whom they executed, now proceeded to divide the garments of the innocent Lamb. The cloak or outside mantle, which by divine disposition they had brought to mount Calvary and which was the one Christ had laid aside at the washing of the feet, thev divided among themselves, cutting it into four parts (John 19,23). But the seamless tunic, by a mysterious decree of Providence, they did not divide, but they drew lots and assigned it entirely to the one who drew the lot for it; thus fulfilling the prophecy in the twentyfirst Psalm. The mysterious signification of the undivided tunic is variously explained by the saints and doctors; one of these explanations being, that though the Jews lacerated and tore with wounds the sacred humanity of Christ our Lord, yet they could not touch or injure the Divinity which was enclosed in the sacred humanity; and whoever should draw the lot of justification by partaking of his Divinity, should thenceforward possess and enjoy it entirely.

As the wood of the Cross was the throne of hi5 majesty and the chair of the doctrine of life, and as He was now raised upon it, confirming his doctrine by his example, Christ now uttered those words of highest charity and perfection: "Father, forgive them, for they know not what they do!" (Luke 23, 34.) This principle of charity and fraternal love the divine Teacher had appropriated to Himself and proclaimed by his own lips (John 15, 12; Matthew IS, 44). He now confirmed and executed it upon the Cross, not only pardoning and loving his enemies, but excusing those under the plea of ignorance whose malice had reached the highest point possible to men in persecuting, blaspheming and crucifying their God and Redeemer. Such was the difference between the behavior of ungrateful men favored with so great enlightenment, instruction and blessing; and the behavior of Jesus in his most burning charity while suffering the crown of thorns. the nails, and the Cross and unheard of blasphemy at the hands of men. O incomprehensible love! O ineffable sweetness! O patience inconceivable to man, admirable to the angels and fearful to the devils! One of the two thieves, called Dismas, became aware of some of the mysteries. Being assisted it the same time by the prayers and intercession of most holy Mary, he was interiorly enlightened concerning lis Rescuer and Master by the first word on the Cross. Moved by true sorrow and contrition for his sins, he turned to his companion and said: "Neither dost thou fear God, seeing that thou art under the same condemnation? And we indeed justly, for we receive the due reward of our deeds; but this Man hath done no evil." And thereupon speaking to Jesus, he said: "Lord, remember me when Thou shalt come into thy kingdom!" (Luke 23, 40.) In this happiest of thieves, in the centurion, and in the others who confessed Jesus Christ on the Cross, began to appear the results of the Redemption. But the one most favored was this Dismas, who merited to hear the second word of the Savior on the Cross: "Amen, I say to thee, this day shalt thou be with Me in Paradise." O fortunate thief, who, of all others, heard those words so much desired by all the saints and just of the earth! Such a word the ancient Patriarchs and Prophets did not hear;

they had judged themselves very happy to be allowed to descend into limbo and wait through the long ages for paradise, which thou, in changing so happily thy condition, didst acquire in one moment. Thou hast now ceased to rob earthly possessions of thy neighbor, and immediately snatchest heaven from the hands of thy Master. Thou seizest it in justice and He yields it to thee in grace, since thou wast the last disciple of his doctrine on earth and the most alert of all in practicing it after having heard it from his mouth. Thou hast lovingly corrected thy brother, confessed thy Creator, reprehended those who blasphemed Him, imitated Him in patient suffering, asked Him humbly as thy Redeemer not to forget thy miseries; and He, as thy Exalter, has at once fulfilled thy desires without delaying the guerdon merited for thee and all the mortals.

Having thus justified the good thief, Jesus turned his loving gaze upon his afflicted Mother, who with saint John was standing at the foot of the Cross. Speaking to both, he first addressed his Mother, saying: "Woman, behold thy son!" and then to the Apostle: "Behold thy Mother !" (John 19, 26.) The Lord called Her Woman and not Mother, because this name of Mother had in it something of sweetness and consolation, the very pronouncing of which would have been a sensible relief. During his Passion He would admit of no exterior consolation, having renounced for that time all exterior alleviation and easement, as I have mentioned above. By this word "woman" he tacitly and by implication wished to say: Woman blessed among all women, the mDst prudent among all the daughters of Adam, Woman, strong and constant, unconquered by any fault of thy own, unfailing in my service and most faithful in thy love toward Me, which even the mighty waters of my Passion could not extinguish or resist (Canticles 8, 7), I am going to my Father and cannot accompany Thee further; my beloved disciple will attend upon Thee and serve Thee as his Mother, and he will be thy son. All this the heavenly Queen understood. The holy Apostle on his part received Her as his own from that hour on; for he was enlightened anew in order to understand and appreciate the greatest treasure of the Divinity in the whole creation next to the humanity of Christ our Savior. In this light He reverenced and served Her for the rest of her life, as I will relate farther on. Our Lady also accepted him as her son in humble subjection and obedience. Always practicing the highest possible perfection and holiness without failing on any occasion, and not permitting even the immensity of her present suffering to weigh down her magnanimous and most prudent heart, She promised then and there that She would show him this obedience during her whole life. Already the ninth hour of the day was approaching, although the darkness and confusion of nature made it appear to be rather a chaotic night. Our Savior spoke the fourth word from the Cross in a loud and strong voice, so that all the bystanders could hear it: "My God, my God, why hast thou forsaken Me?" (Matthew 27, 46.) Although the Lord had uttered these words in his own Hebrew language, they were not understood by all. Since they began with: "Eli, eli," some of them thought He was calling upon Elias, and a number of them rqocked Him saying: "Let us see whether Elias shall come to free Him from our hands?" But the mystery concealed beneath these words was just as profound as it was unintelligible to the Jews and gentiles; and they have been interpreted in many ways by the doctors of the Church. I shall give the interpretation which has been manifested to me. The dereliction of which Christ speaks, was not one in which the Divinity separated from the humanity, dissolving the hypostatic union, nor including a cessation of the beatific vision in his soul; for both of these He enjoyed from the first moment of his conception by the Holy Ghost in the virginal womb and could never lose. But certainly the sacred humanity was in so far forsaken by the Divinity as it did not ward off death or the most bitter sorrows of his Passion; though, on the other hand, the eternal Father did not forsake Him entirely, since He showed his concern by causing the changes in the visible creation in order to give witness for his honor at his Death. Christ our Savior intimated quite a different dereliction by these words of complaint. one which originated from his immense love for men; namely, from his love of the foreknown as lost and the reprobate, which during his last hour caused in Him the same anguish as it did during his prayer in the garden. He grieved that his copious and superabundant Redemption, offered for the whole human race, should not be efficacious in the reprobate and that He should find Himself deprived of them in the eternal happiness, for which He had created and redeemed them. As this was to happen in consequence of the decree of his Father's eternal will, He lovingly and sorrowfully complained of it in the words: "My God, my God, why hast Thou forsaken Me?" that is, in so far as God deprived Him of the salvation of the reprobate.

In confirmation of this sorrow the Lord added: "I thirst!" The sufferings of the Lord and his anguish could easily cause a natural thirst. But for Him this was not a time to complain of this thirst or to quench it; and therefore Jesus would not have spoken of it so near to its expiration, unless in order to give expression to a most exalted mystery. He was thirsting to see the captive children of Adam make use of the liberty, which He merited for them and offered to them, and which so many were abusing. He was athirst with the anxious desire that all should correspond with Him in the faith and love due to Him, that they profit by his merits and sufferings, accept his friendship and grace now acquired for them, and that they should not lose the eternal happiness which He was to leave as an inheritance to those that wished to merit and accept it. This was the thirst of our Savior and Master; and the most blessed Mary alone understood it perfectly and began, with ardent 1ffection and charity, to invite and interiorly to call upon 111 the poor, the afflicted, the humble, the despised and downtrodden to approach their Savior and thus quench, at least in part, his thirst which they could not quench entirely. But the perfidious Jews and the executioners, evidencing their unhappy hardheartedness, fastened a sponge soaked in gall and vinegar to a reed and mockingly raised it to his mouth, in order that He might drink of it. Thus was fulfilled the prophecy of David: "In my thirst they gave me vinegar to drink" (John 16, 28; Psalms 68, 22). Our most patient Savior tasted of it, partaking of this drink in mysterious submission to the condemnation of the reprobate. But at the instance of his blessed Mother He immediately desisted; because the Mother of grace was to be the portal and Mediatrix of those who were to profit of the Passion and the Redemption of mankind.

In connection with this same mystery the Savior then pronounced the sixth word: "Consummatum est," "It is consummated" (John 19, 29). Now is consummated this work of my coming from heaven and I have obeyed the command of my eternal Father, who sent Me to suffer and die for the salvation of mankind. Now are fulfilled the holy Scriptures, the prophecies and figures of the old Testament, and the course of my earthly and mortal life assumed in the womb of my Mother. Now are established on earth my example, my doctrines, my Sacraments and my remedies for the sickness of sin. Now is appeased the justice of my eternal Father in regard to the debt of the children of Adam. Now is my holy Church enriched with the remedies for the sins committed by men; the whole work of my coming into the world is perfected in so far as concerns Me, its Restorer; the secure foundation of the triumphant Church is now laid in the Church militant, so that nothing can overthrow or change it. These are the mysteries contained in the few words: "Consummatum est."

Having finished and established the work of Redemption in all its perfection, it was becoming that the incarnate Word, just as He came forth from the Father to enter mortal life (John 16, 8), should enter into immortal life of the Father through death. Therefore Christ our Savior added the last words uttered by Him: "Father, into thy hands I commend my spirit." The Lord spoke these words in a loud and strong voice, so that the bystanders heard them. In pronouncing them He raised his eyes to heaven, as one speaking with the eternal Father, and with the last accent He gave up his spirit and inclined his head. By the divine force of these words Lucifer with all his demons were hurled into the deepest caverns of hell, there they lay motionless, as I shaH relate in the next chapter. The invincible Queen and Mistress of all virtues understood these mysteries beyond the understanding of all creatures, as She was the Mother of the Savior and the Coadjutrix of his Passion. In order that She might participate in it to the end, just as She had felt in her own body the other torments of her Son, She now, though remaining alive, felt and suffered the pangs and agony of his death. She did not die in reality; but this was because God miraculously preserved her life, when according to the natural course death should have followed. This miraculous aid was more wonderful than all the other favors She received during the Passion. For this last pain was more intense and penetrating; and all that the martyrs and the men sentenced to death have suffered from the beginning of the world cannot equal what the blessed Mary suffered during the Passion. The great Lady remained at the foot of the Cross until evening, when the sacred body (as I shall relate) was interred. But in return for this last anguish of death, all that was still of this mortal life in the virginal body of the purest Mother, was more than ever exalted and spiritualized.

688. Of many of the sacraments and mysteries connected with the doings of Christ our Savior on the Cross the Evangelists make no mention; and we as Catholics can only form prudent conjectures founded upon the infallible certainty of our faith. But among those which have been manifested to me in this history, and concerning this part of the Passion, is a prayer, which Christ addressed to his eternal Father before speaking the seven words on the Cross recorded by the Evangelists. I call it a prayer because it was addressed to the Father; but in reality it was a last bequest or testament, which He made as a true and most wise Father in order to consign his possessions to his family, that is, to the whole human race. Even natural reason teaches us, that he who is the head of a family or the lord over many or few

possessions, would not be a prudent dispenser of his goods, and inattentive to his office or dignity, if at the hour of his death he would not make known his will in regard to the disposition of his goods and his estate, in order that each one of his family may know what belongs to him and may possess it justly and peacefully without recourse to lawsuits. For this very reason, and in order that they may set their minds at ease in preparation for the hour of death, men of the world make their last testaments. And even the religious resign the things permitted them for daily use, because in that hour earthly matters are apt to fill the mind with anxieties and prevent them from rising toward their Creator. Although earthly things could not disturb our Savior, since He neither possessed them, nor, if He had possessed any, could He be embarrassed by them in his infinite power; yet it was fitting, that He should in that hour dispose of the spiritual riches and treasures which He had amassed for mankind in the course of his pilgrimage.

Of these eternal goods the Savior made his last disposition on the Cross, distributing them and pointing out those who should be legitimate heirs and those who should be disinherited, and mentioning the reasons for the one as well as the other. All this He did in conference with his eternal Father, as the supreme Lord and most just Judge of all creatures; for in this testament are rehearsed the mysteries of the predestination of the saints and of the reprobation of the wicked. It was a testament hidden and sealed for mankind; only the blessed Mary understood it, because, in addition to her being informed of the operations of the divine Soul of Christ, She was also to be the universal Heiress of all creation. As She was the Coadjutrix of salvation, She was also to be the testamentary Executrix. For the Son placed all things in her hands, just as the Father had assigned the whole creation to Him. She was to execute his will and she was to distribute all the treasures acquired and due to her Son as God on account of his infinite merits. This understanding has been given me as part of this history for the exaltation of our Queen and in order that sinners might approach Her as the Custodian of all the treasures gained by her Son and our Redeemer in the sight of his eternal Father. All help and assistance is in the hands of most holy Mary and She is to distribute it according to her most sweet kindness and liberality.

Testament Made By Christ Our Lord On the Cross

In His Prayer to the Eternal Father

When the holy wood of the Cross had been raised on mount Calvary, bearing aloft with it the incarnate Word crucified before speaking any of the seven words, Christ prayed interiorly to his heavenly Father and said: "My Father and eternal God, I confess and magnify Thee from this tree of the Cross, and I offer Thee a sacrifice of praise in my Passion and Death; for, by the hypostatic union with the divine nature, Tholl hast raised my humanity to the highest dignity, that of Christ, the God-man, anointed with thy own Divinity. I confess Thee on account of the plenitude of the highest possible graces and glory, which from the first instant of my Incarnation Thou hast communicated to my humanity, and because from all eternity up to this present hour Thou hast consigned to me full dominion of the universe both in the order of grace and of nature. Thou hast made Me the Lord of the heavens and of the elements (Matthew 28, 18). of the sun, the moon and the stars; of fire and air, of the earth and the sea, of all the animate and inanimate creatures therein; Thou hast made Me the Disposer of the seasons, of the days and nights, with full lordship and possession according to my free will, and Thou hast set Me as the Head, the King and Lord of all angels and men (Ephes. 1,21). to govern and command them, to punish the wicked and to reward the good (John 5, 22) ; Thou hast given Me the dominion and power of disposing all things from highest heavens to deepest abysses of hell (Apocalypse 20, 1). Thou hast placed in my hands the eternal justification of men, the empires, kingdoms and principalities, the great and the little. the rich and the poor; and of all that are capable of thy grace and glory, Thou hast made Me the Justifier, the Redeemer and Glorifier, the universal Lord of all the human race. of life and death, of the holy Church. its treasures, laws and blessings of grace: all hast Thou, my Father, consigned to my hands, subjected to my will and my decrees, and for this I confess, exalt and magnify thy holy name."

"Now, at this moment, my Lord and eternal Father, when I am returning from this world to thy right hand through this death on the Cross, by which I completed the task of the Redemption of men assigned to Me, I desire that this same Cross shall be the tribunal of our justice and mercy. Nailed to it, I desire to judge those for whom I give my life. Having justified my cause, I wish to dispense the treasures of my coming into the world and of my Passion and Death to the just and the reprobate according as each one merits by his works of love or hatred. I have sought to gain all mortals and invited them to partake of my friendship and grace; from the first moment of my Incarnation I have ceaselessly labored for them; I have borne inconveniences, fatigues, insults, ignominies, reproaches, scourges, a crown of thorns, and now suffer the bitter death of the Cross; I have implored thy vast kindness upon all of them; I have watched in prayer, fasted and wandered about teaching them the way of eternal life. As far as in Me lay I have sought to secure eternal happiness for all men, just as I merited it for all, without excluding anyone. I have established and built up the law of grace and have firmly and forever established the Church in which all human beings can be saved."

"But in our knowledge and foresight We are aware, my God and Father, that on account of their malice and rebellious obstinacy not all men desire to ~ccept our eternal salvation, nor avail themselves of Jur mercy and of the way I have opened to them by my :abors, life and death; but that many will prefer to follow their sinful ways unto perdition. Thou art just, ny Lord and Father, and most equitable are thy judgments (Psalms 68, 13); and therefore it is right, since Thou hast made Me the Judge of the living and the dead, of the good and the bad (Act 10, 3), that I give to the good the reward of having served and followed Me, and to sinners the chastisement of their perverse obstinacy; that the just should share in my goods, and the wicked he deprived of the inheritance, which they refuse to accept. Now then, my eternal Father, in my and thy name and for thy glorification, I make my last bequest according to my human will, which is conformable to thy eternal and divine will. First shall be mentioned my most pure Mother, who gave Me human existence; Her I constitute my sole and universal Heiress of all the gifts of nature, of grace and of glory that are mine. She shall be Mistress and Possessor of them all. The gifts of grace, of which as a mere creature She is capable, She shall actually receive now, while those of glory I promise to confer upon Her in their time. I desire that She shall be Mistress of angels and men, claim over them full possession and dominion and command the service and obedience of all. The demons shall fear Her and be subject to Her. All the irrational creatures, the heavens, the stars, the planets, the elements with all the living beings, the birds, the fishes and the animals contained in them, shall likewise be subject to Her and acknowledge Her as Mistress, exalting and glorifying Her with Me. l wish also that She be the Treasurer and Dispenser of all the goods in heaven and on earth. Whatever She ordains and disposes in my Church for my children, the sons of men, shall be confirmed by the three divine Persons; and whatever She shall ask for mortals now, afterwards and forever, We shall concede according to her will and wishes."

"To the holy angels, who have obeyed thy holy and just will, I assign as habitation the highest heavens as their proper and eternal abode, and with it the joys of eternal vision and fruition of our Divinity. I desire that they enjoy its everlasting possession together with our company and friendship. I decree, that they recognize my Mother as their legitimate Queen and Lady, that they serve Her, accompany and attend upon Her, bear Her up in their hands in all places and times, obeying Her in all that She wishes to ordain and command. The demons, rebellious to our perfect and holy will, I cast out and deprive of our vision and company; again do I condemn them to our abhorrence, to eternal loss of our friendship and glory, to privation of the vision of my Mother, of the saints and of my friends, the just. I appoint and assign to them as their eternal dwelling the place most remote from our royal throne, namely the infernal caverns, the centre of the earth, deprived of light and fun of the horrors of sensible darkness (Jude 6). I decree this to be their portion and inheritance, as chosen by them in their pride and obstinacy against the divine Being and decrees. In those eternal dungeons of darkness they shall be tormented by everlasting and inextinguishable fire."

"From the multitudes of men, in the fulness of my good will, I call, select and separate all the just and the predestined, who through my grace save themselves by imitating Me, doing my will and obeying my holy law. These, next to my most pure Mother, I appoint as the inheritors of all my mysteries, my blessings, my sacramental treasures, of the mysteries concealed in the holy Scriptures; of my humility, meekness of heart; of the virtues of faith, hope, and charity; of prudence, justice, fortitude and temperance; of my divine gifts and favors; of my Cross, labors, contempt, poverty and nakedness. This shall be their portion and inheritance in this present and mortal life. Since they must choose these in order to labor profitably, I assign to them the trials I have chosen for Myself in this life, as a pledge of my friendship, in order that they may undergo them with joy. I offer them my protection and defense, my holy inspirations, my favors and powerful assistance, my blessings and my justification, according to each one's disposition and degree of love. I promise to be to them a Father, a Brother and a Friend, and they shall be my chosen and beloved children, and as such I appoint them as the inheritors of all my merits and treasures without limitation. I desire that all who dispose themselves, shall partake of the goods of my holy Church and of the Sacraments; that, if they should lose my friendship, they shall be able to restore themselves and recover my graces and blessings through my cleansing blood. For all of them shall be open the intercession of my Mother and of the saints, and She shall recognize them as her children, shielding them and holding them as her own. My angels shall defend them, guide them, protect them and bear them up in their hands lest they stumble, and if they fall, they shall help them to rise" (Psalms 90, 11, 12).

"Likewise it is my will that my just and chosen ones shall stand high above the reprobate and the demons, that they shall be feared and obeyed by my enemies; that all the rational and irrational creatures shall serve them; that all the influences of the heavens, the planets and the stars shall favor them and give them life; that the earth, its elements and animals, shall sustain them; all the creatures, that are mine and serve Me, shall be theirs, and shall serve also them as my children and friends (I Corinthians 3, 22; Wisdom 16, 24), and their blessing shall be in the dew of heaven and in the fruits of the earth (Genesis 27, 28). I wish to hold with them my delights (Pros. 8, 31), communicate to them my secrets, converse with them intimately and live with them in the militant Church in the species of bread and wine, as an earnest and an infallible pledge of the eternal happiness and glory promised to them; of it, I make them partakers and heirs, in order that they may enjoy it with Me in heaven by perpetual right and in unfailing beatitude."

"I consent that the foreknown and reprobate (though they were created for another and much higher end), shall be permitted to possess as their portion and inheritance the concupiscence of the flesh and the eyes (John 1, 216), pride in all its effects; that they eat and be satisfied with the dust of the earth, namely, with riches; with the fumes and the corruption of the flesh and its delights, and with the vanity and presumption of the world. For such possessions have they labored, and applied all the diligence of their mind and body; in such occupations have they consumed their powers, their gifts and blessings bestowed upon them by Us, and they have of their own free will chosen deceit, despising the truth I have taught them in the holy law (Romans 2, 8). They have rejected the law which I have written in their hearts and the one inspired by my grace; they have despised my teachings and my blessings, and listened to my and their own enemies; they have accepted their deceits, have loved vanity (Psalms 4, 3), wrought injustice, followed their ambitions, sought their delight in vengeance, persecuted the poor, humiliated the just, mocked the simple and the innocent, strove to exalt themselves and desired to be raised above all the cedars of Lebanon in following the laws of injustice" (Psalms 36, 35).

"Since they have done all this in opposition in our divine goodness and remained obstinate in their malice, and since they have renounced the rights of sonship merited for them by Me, I disinherit them of my friendship and glory. Just as Abraham separated the children of the slave, setting aside some possessions for them and reserving the principal heritage for Isaac, the son of the freedwoman Sarah (Genesis 25, 5), thus I set aside their claims on my inheritance by giving them the transitory goods, which they themselves have chosen. Separating them from our company and from that of my Mother, of the angels and saints, I condemn them to the eternal dungeons and the fire of hell in the company of Lucifer and his demons, whom they have freely served, I deprive them forever of all hope of relief. This is, O my Father, the sentence which I pronounce as the Head and the Judge of men and angels (Ephesians 4, 15; Colossians 2. 10). and this is the testament made at my Death, this is the effect of my Redemption, whereby each one is rewarded with that which he has justly merited according to his works and according to thy incomprehensible wisdom in the equity of thy strictest justice" (II Timothy 4, 8). Such was the prayer of Christ our Savior on the Cross to his eternal Father. It was sealed and deposited in the heart of the most holy :'.fary as the mysterious and sacramental testament, in order that through her intercession and solicitous care it might at its time. and even from that moment, be executed in the Church. just as it had before this time been prepared and perfected by the wise providence of God, in whom all the past and the future is always one with the present.

Instruction, which Mary, the Queen of Heaven Gave Me

698. My daughter, seek with all the powers of thy mind during thy whole life to remember the mysteries manifested to thee in this chapter. I, as thy Mother and thy Instructress, shall ask the Lord by his divine power to impress in thy heart the knowledge. which I have vouchsafed thee, in order that it may remain fixed and ever present to thee as long as thou livest. In virtue of this blessing keep in thy memory Christ crucified. who is my divine Son and thy Spouse, and

never forget the sufferings of the Cross and the doctrine taught by Him upon it. This is the mirror by which thou must arrange all thy adornments and the source from which thou art to draw thy interior beauty, like a true daughter of the Prince (Psalms 44, 14). in order that thou mayest be prepared, proceed and reign as the spouse of the supreme King. As this honorable title obliges thee to seek with all thy power to imitate Him as far as is becoming thy station and possible to thee by his grace, and as this is to be the true fruit of my doctrine, I wish that from today on thou live crucified with Christ, entirely assimilated to thy exemplar and model and dead to this earthly life (II Corinthians 5, 15). I desire that in thee shall vanish ~he effects of the first sin, that thou live only for the Jperations and movements of divine virtue, and that :hou renounce thy inheritance as a daughter of the first Adam, in order that in thee may bear fruit the inheritance of the second Adam, who is Jesus Christ. thy Redeemer and Teacher.

Thy state of life must be for thee a most rigid cross on which thou must remain crucified, and thou must not widen thy path by seeking for dispensation and weakening interpretation of thy rules to make it easy and com fortable, but at the same time, insecure and full of imperfections. This is the deception into which the children of Babylon and of Adam fall, that each one according to his state seeks to find ease in the work commanded by the law of God. They set aside the salvation of their soul in their efforts to buy heaven very cheaply, or risk losing it by dreading the restrictions and entire subjection necessary to observe rigorously the divine law and its precepts. Hence arises the desire to find explanations and opinions, which smooth the paths and highways of eternal life, without heeding the doctrine of my divine Son, that the path of life is very narrow (Matth. 7, 14). They forget that the Lord himself has walked these narrow paths, in order that no one might imagine he can reach eternal Ii fe over paths more spacious and comfortable to the flesh and to the inclinations vitiated by sins. This danger is greater for ecclesiastics and religious, who by their very state must follow the Master and must accommodate themselves to his Ii fe of poverty and must choose for this purpose the way of the Cross. Some of them however are apt to seek the dignities attached to the religious state for their temporal advantage, for the increase of their own honor and praise. In order to secure it they lighten the Cross they have promised to bear, so that they live a carnal life, little restricted and much eased by deceptive dispensations and vain excuses. l n their time they shall recognize the truth and that saying of the Holy Ghost: Each one thinks his path secure, but the Lord weighs in his hands the hearts of men (Proverbs 21, 2).

So far from this deceit, do I wish thee to be, my daughter, that thou must live strictly up to the most rigorous demands of thy profession; in such a way that thou canst not stretch thyself in any way, being nailed immovably to the Cross with Christ. Thou must set aside all temporal advantages, for the least' point pertaining to the utmost perfection of thy state. Thy right hand, my daughter, must be nailed to the Cross by obedience, and reserve not for thyself the least movement, the least activity, or word, or thought not controlled by this virtue. Thou must not maintain any position that is of thy own choice, but only such as is willed by others; thou must not appear wise in thy own conceit in anything, but ignorant and blind, in order to follow entirely the guidance of thy superiors (Proverbs 3, 7). He that promises, says the wise man (Proverbs 6, I), binds his hands, and by his words shall he be bound and chained. Thou hast bound thy hand by the vow of obedience and hast thereby lost thy liberty and thy right of wishing or not wishing. Thy left hand thou hast nailed to the Cross by the vow of poverty, depriving thee of all right to follow any inclination toward the objects usually coveted by the eyes; for both in the use and in the desire for such creatures thou must rigorously imitate Christ impoverished and despoiled upon the Cross. By the third vow. that of chastity, thy feet are nailed to the Cross, in order that all thy steps and movements may be pure, chaste and beautiful. For this thou must not permit in thy presence the least word offensive to purity, nor, by looking upon or touching any human creature, allow any sensual image or impression within thee; thy eyes and all thy senses are to remain consecrated to chastity, without making more use of them than to fix them upon Jesus crucified. The fourth vow, of perpetual enclosure, thou wilt maintain in the bosom of my divine Son, to which I consign thee. In order that this doctrine may appear to thee sweet, and this path less narrow, contemplate and consider in thy heart the image of my Son and Lord full of blood, torments, sorrows, and at last nailed to the Cross, no part of his sacred body being exempt from wounds and excruciating pains. The Lord and I were most solicitous and compassionate toward all the children of men; for them We suffered and endured such bitter sorrows, in order that they might be encouraged not to refuse less severe sufferings for their own eternal good and in return for so obliging a love. Therefore let mortals show themselves thankful, willingly entering upon the rough and thorny path and accepting the Cross, to bear it after Christ. Thus will they walk upon the direct path toward heaven and gain an eternal happiness (Matthew 16,24).

The Triumph of Christ Our Saviour Over the Demon on the Cross

His Death and the Prophecy of Habbucuc; The Council of the Demons in Hell.

The hidden and venerable mysteries of this chapter correspond to many others scattered through the whole extent of this history. One of them is, that Lucifer and his demons in the course of the life and miracles of our Savior, never could ascertain fully whether the Lord was true God and Redeemer of the world, and coosequently what was the dignity of the most holy Mary. This was so disposed by divine Providence, in order that the whole mystery of the Incarnation and the Redemption of the human race might be more fittingly accomplished. Lucifer, although knowing that God was to assume human flesh, nevertheless knew nothing of the manner and the circumstances of the Incarnation. As he was permitted to form an opinion of this mystery in accordance with his pride, he was full of hallucinations, sometimes believing Christ to be God on account of his miracles, sometimes rejecting such an opinion on account of seeing Him poor, humiliated, afflicted and fatigued. Harassed by these contradicting evidences, he remained in doubt and continued his inquiries until the predestined hour of Christ's Death on the Cross, where, in virtue of the Passion and Death of the sacred humanity, which he had himself brought about, he was to be both undeceived and vanquished by the full solution of these mysteries.

This triumph of Christ our Savior was accomplished in such an exalted and miraculous manner, that I feel the sluggishness and insufficiency of my powers to describe it. It took place in a manner too spiritual and too far removed from the perception of the senses, . according to which I must describe its process. In order to manifest it, I should wish we were able to speak and understand one another by means of the simple intercourse and vision peculiar to the angels; for such would bc necessary in order to describe and understand correctly this great miracle of the omnipotence of God. I shall say what I can and leave the understanding of it more to the enlightenment of faith than to the signification of my words.

In the preceding chapter I have said that Lucifer and his demons, as soon as they saw the Lord taking the Cross upon his sacred shoulders, wished to fly and cast themselves into hell; for at that moment they began to feel with greater force the operations of his divine power. By divine intervention this new torment made them aware that the Death of this innocent Man, whose destruction they had plotted and who could not be a mere man, threatened great ruin to themselves. They therefore desired to withdraw and they ceased to incite the Jews and the executioners, as they had done hitherto. But the command of the most blessed Mary, enforced by the divine power, detained them and, enchained like fiercest dragons. compelled them to accompany Christ to Calvary. The ends of the mysterious chain that bound them were placed into the hands of Mary, the great Queen, who, by the power of her divine Son, held them all in subjection and bondage. Although they many times sought to break away and raged in helpless fury, they could not overcome the power of the heavenly Lady. She forced them to come to Calvary and stand around the Cross, where She commanded them to remain motionless and witness the end of the great mysteries there enacted for the salvation of men and the ruin of themselves.

Lucifer and his infernal hosts were so overwhelmed with pains and torments by the presence of the Lord and his blessed Mother, and with the fear of their impending ruin, that they would have felt greatly relieved to be allowed to cast themselves into the darkness of hell. As this was not permitted them, they fell upon one another and furiously fought with each other like hornets disturbed in their nest, or like a brood of vermin confusedly seeking some dark shelter. But their rabid fury was not that of animals, but that of demons more cruel than dragons. Then the haughty pride of Lucifer saw itself entirely vanquished and all his proud thoughts of setting his throne above the stars of heaven and drinking dry the waters of the Jordan put to shame (Isaias 14, 13; Job 40, 18). How weak and annihilated was now he, who so often had presumed to overturn the whole earth! How downcast and can founded he. who had deceived so many souls by false promises and "ain threats! How dismayed this unhappy one at the sight of the gibbet, where he had sought to place Mardocheus! (Esther 7, 9). What horrid shame to see the true Esther, most holy Mary, asking for the rescue of her people and the downfall of the traitor and the chastisement of his pride! There our invincible Judith beheaded him (Judith 13, 10); there She trod upon his haughty neck. From now on, O Lucifer, I know that thy arrogance and pride is much greater than thy strength (Isaias 16.6). Instead of splendor now worms clothe thee about (Isaias 14, 11), and rottenness envelops and consumes thy carrion corpse! Thou, who hast afflicted the nations, art now more wounded, bound and oppressed than all the world. Thenceforward I do not fear thy counterfeit threats; I will no longer listen to thy wiles; for I see thee reduced, weakened and entirely helpless.

The time had now come for this ancient dragon to be vanquished by the Master of life. As this was to be the hour of his disillusionment, and as this poisonous asp was not to escape it by stopping his ears to the voice of the Enchanter (Psalms 57, 5), the Lord began to speak the seven words from his Cross, at the same time providing that Lucifer and his demons should understand the mysteries therein contained. For it was by this disclosure that the Lord wished to triumph over them, over sin and death, and despoil them of their tyrannous power over the human race. The Savior then pronounced the first word: "Father, forgive them, for they know not what they do!" (Luke 23, 34). By these words the princes of darkness came to the full conviction, that Christ our Lord was speaking to the eternal Father, that He was his natural Son and the true God with Him and the Holy Ghost, that He had permitted death in hi, most sacred and perfect humanity, united to the Divinity for the salvation of the whole human race; that now He offered his infinitely precious· merits for the pardon of the sins of all those children of Adam, who should avail themselves thereof for their rescue, not excepting even the wretches that crucified Him. At this discovery Lucifer and his demons were thrown into such fury and despair that they instantly wished to hurl themselves impetuously to the depths of hell and strained all their powers to accomplish it in spite of the powerful Queen.

In the second word spoken by the Lord to the fortunate thief: "Amen I say to thee, today thou shalt he with Me in paradise," the demons understood that the fruits of the Redemption in the justification of sinners ended in the glorification of the just. They were made aware that from this hour the merits of Christ would commence to act with a new force and strength, that through them should be opened the gates of Paradise, which had been closed by the first sin, and that from now on men would enter upon eternal happiness and occupy their destined heayenly seats, which until now had heen impossible for them. They perceived the power of Christ to call sinners, justify and beautify them, and they felt the triumphs gained over themselves by the exalted virtues, the humility, patience, meekness and all the virtues of his life. The confusion and torment of Lucifer at seeing this cannot be explained by human tongue; but it was so great, that he humiliated himself so far as to beg the most blessed Virgin to permit them to descend into hell and be cast out from her presence; hut the great Queen would not consent, as the time had not yet arrived.

At the third word spoken by the Lord to his Mother: "Woman, behold thy son!" the demons discvered that this heavenly Lady was the true Mother of the God-man, the same Woman whose likeness and prophetic sign had been shown to them in the heavens. at their creation, and who was to crush their head as announced by the Lord in the terrestrial paradise. They were informed of the dignity and excellence of this great Lady over all creatures, and of her power which they were even now experiencing. As they had from the beginning of the world and from the creation of the first woman, used all their astuteness to find out who this great woman that was announced in the heavens could be, and as they now discovered Her in Mary, whom they had until now overlooked, these dragons were seized with inexpressible fury; their having been thus mistaken crushed their arrogance beyond all their other torments, and in their fury they raged against their own selves like bloodthirsty lions, while their helpless wrath against the heavenly Lady was increased a thousandfold. Moreover, they discerned that saint John was appointed by Christ our Lord as the angel guardian of his Mother, endowed with the powers of the priesthood. This they understood to be in the nature of a threat against their own wrath, which was well known to saint John. Lucifer saw not only the power of the Evangelist, but that given to all the priests in virtue of their participation in the dignity and power of our Redeemer; and that the rest of the just, even though no priests, were placed under the special protection of the Lord and made powerful against hell. All this paralyzed the strength of Lucifer and his demons.

The fourth word of Christ was addressed to the eternal Father: "God, my God, why hast Thou forsaken Me?" The evil spirits discovered in these words that the charity of God toward men was boundless and everlasting; that, in order to satisfy it, He had mysteriously suspended the influence of the Divinity over his most sacred humanity, thus permitting his sufferings to reach the highest degree and drawing from them the most abundant fruits; that He was aware and lovingly complained of his being deprived of the salvation of a part of the human race; how ready He was to suffer more, if such would be ordained by the eternal Father. Man's good fortune in being so beloved by God increased the envy of Lucifer and his demons, and they foresaw the divine Omnipotence following out this immense love without limitation. This knowledge crushed the haughty malice of the enemies and they were made welJ aware of their own weakness and helplessness in opposing this love, if men themselves should not choose to neglect its influence.

The fifth word of Christ, "I thirst," confirmed Christ's triumph over the devil and his followers; they were filled with wrath and fury because the Lord clearly let them see their total overthrow. By these words they understood Him to say to them: If what I suffer for men and my love for them seem great to you, be assured that my love for them is still unsatiated, that it continues to long for their eternal salvation, and that the mighty waters of torments and sufferings have not extinguished it (Canticles 8, 7). Much more would I suffer for them, if it were necessary, in order to deliver them from your tyranny and make them powerful and strong against your malice and pride.

In the sixth word of the Lord: "It is consummated!" Lucifer and his hordes were informed that the mystery of the Incarnation and Redemption was now accomplished and entirely perfected according to the decree of divine wisdom. For they were made to feel that Christ our Redeemer had obediently fulfilled the will of the eternal Father: that He had accomplished alJ the promises and prophecies made to the world by the ancient Fathers; that his humility and obedience had compensated for their own pride and disobedience in heaven in not having subjected themselves and acknowledged Him as their Superior in human flesh; and that they were now through the wisdom of God justly humbled and vanquished by the very Lord whom they despised. The great dignity and the infinite merits of Christ demanded that in this very hour He should exercise his office and power of Judge over angels and men, such as had been conceded to Him by the eternal Father. He now applied this power by hurling this sentence at Lucifer and all his followers, that, being condemned to eternal fire, they instantly depart into the deepest dungeons of hell. This very sentence was included in the pronouncing of the seventh word: "Father, into thy hands I commend my spirit!n (Luke 23, 46.) The mighty Queen and Mother concurred with the will of her Son Jesus and united with his her command that Lucifer and all demons depart to the infernal depths. In virtue of these decrees of the supreme King and of the Queen, the evil spirits were routed from Calvary and precipitated to deepest hell more violently and suddenly than a flash of light through the riven clouds.

Christ our Savior, as the triumphant Conqueror having vanquished the great enemy, now yielded up his spirit to the Father and permitted death to approach by inclining his head (John 19,30). By this permission He also vanquished death, which had been equally deceived in Him with the demons. For death could not attack men, or had any jurisdiction of them, except through the first sin, of which it was a punishment. On this account the Apostle says that the weapon or the sting of death is sin, which opens up the wounds by which death enters into the world of humanity (Romans 5, 12); and as our Savior paid the debt of sin which He could not commit, therefore, when death took away his life without the shadow of justice, it lost the power which it had over the other sons of Adam (I Corinthians 15,55). Thenceforward neither death nor the devil could attack men, unless they,

failing to avail themselves of the victory of Christ, should again subject themselves of their own free will. If our first Father Adam had not sinned and we ourselves in him, we would not suffer the punishment of death, but merely pass over to the happiness of the eternal fatherland. But sin has made us its subjects and slaves of the devil. He avails himself of death to deprive us first of the grace, the blessings and the friendship of God. Thereby he also prevents us from reaching eternal life and we remain in the slavery of sin and the devil, subject to his tyrannous power (I John 3, 8). Our Savior Christ despoiled the demon of all these advantages and, in dying without sin and satisfying for our own, merited that our death should be a death of the body only, and not of the soul; that it should have power to take away our temporal life, but not our eternal; the natural, not the spiritual; and that it should thenceforward be merely the portal to the eternal happiness, if we ourselves did not renounce that blessing. Thus the Lord satisfied for the chastisements due to the first sin, at the same time furnishing us a means of offering a compensation in our own name by accepting our natural and bodily death for the love of God. Christ absorbed death (I Corinthians 15,51) and offered his own as a bait for deceiving death (Osee. 13, 14). By his Death He put an end of its power, overcame it, and was the Death of death itself.

In this triumph the Savior fulfilled the prophecy contained in the canticle and prayer of Habbacuc, of which I shall select some passages necessary for my purpose. The prophet was informed of the mystery and the power of Christ over death and the devil. In prophetic foresight he prayed that the Lord vivify the work of his hands, that is, man; that in his greatest wrath He remember his mercy. He prophesied that the glory of this miracle should fill the heavens and the praise of it, the earth; that its splendor shall be as that of light; that in his hands lIe shall embrace the horns, which are the arms of the Cross and wherein is hidden his strength; that death should fly from Him captive and vanquished; that before his feet the devil should be routed and measure the earth (Habacuc 3, 25). All this was fulfilled to the letter; for Lucifer departed having his head crushed under the feet of Christ and his blessed Mother, who subdued Him by their sufferings and by their power. Since the devil was forced to cast himself to lowest hell, which is the middle of the earth and farthest removed from its surface, he is said to measure the earth. The rest of the canticle pertains to the triumph of Christ our Lord in the succeeding ages of the Church; but that need not be rehearsed here. It is, however, proper for men to understand that Lucifer and his demons were restricted, lamed and weakened in their power of tempting the rational creatures, unless their sins and their own free will do not again unbind them and encourage them to return for the destruction of the world. All this will be better understood from the proceedings of the infernal council held in hell and from what I shall say further in the course of this history.

Council Held By Lucipher And His Demons In Hell After the Deatrh of Christ Our Lord

The rout of Lucifer and his angels from Calvary to the abyss of hell was more violent and disastrous than their first expulsion from heaven. Though, as holy Job says (Job 10, 21), that place is a land of darkness, covered with the shades of death, full of gloomy disorder, misery, torments and confusion; yet on this occasion the chaos and disorder was a thousandfold increased; because the damned were made to feel new horror and additional punishments at the sudden meeting of the ferocious demons in their rabid fury. It is certain that the devils have not the power of assigning the damned to a place of greater or lesser torment; for all their torments are decreed by divine justice according to the measure of the demerits of each of the condemned. But, besides this essential punishment, the just Judge allows them to suffer other accidental punishments from time to time according to occasion; for their sins have left roots in the world and cause much damage to others, who are damned on their account, and the new effects still arising from fanner sins cause such accidental punishments in the damned. Thus the demons devised new tonnents for Judas, for having sold and brought about the death of Christ. They also understood then that this place of dreadful punishments, where they had thrown him and of which I have spoken above, was destined for the chastisement of those who damned themselves by refusing to practice their faith in their lives and for those who purposely refuse to believe and avail themselves of the fruits of the Redemption. Against these the devils execute a more furious wrath, similar to the one they have conceived against Jesus and Mary.

As soon as Lucifer was permitted to proceed in these matters and arise from the consternation in which he remained for some time, he set about proposing to his fellow demons new plans of his pride. For this purpose he called them all together and placing himself in an elevated position, he spoke to them: "To you, who have for so many ages followed and still follow my standards for the vengeance of my wrongs, is known the injury which I have now sustained at the hands of this Man God, and how for thirtythree years He has led me about in deceit, hiding his Divinity and concealing the operations of his soul, and how He has now triumphed over us by the very Death which we have brought upon Him. Before He assumed flesh I hated Him and refused to acknowledge Him as being more worthy than I to be adored by the rest of creation. Although on account of this resistance I was cast out from heaven with you and was degraded to this abominable condition so unworthy of my greatness and former beauty, I am even more tormented to see mysel f thus vanquished and oppressed by this Man and by his Mother. From the day on which the first man was created I have sleeplessly sought to find Them and destroy Them; or if I should not be able to destroy Them, I at least wished to bring destruction upon all his creatures and induce them not to acknowledge Him as their God, and that none of them should ever draw any benefit from his works. This has been my intent, to this all my solicitude and efforts were directed. But in vain, since He has overcome me by his humility and poverty, crushed me by his patience, and at last has despoiled me of the sovereignty of the world by his Passion and frightful Death. This causes me such an excruciating pain, that, even if I succeeded in hurling Him from the right hand of his Father, where He sits triumphant, and if I should draw all the souls redeemed down into this hell, my wrath would not be satiated or my fury placated."

"Is it possible that the human nature, so inferior to my own, shall be exalted above all the creatures! That it should be so loved and favored, as to be united to the Creator in the person of the eternal Word! That He should first make war upon me before executing this work, and afterwards overwhelm me with such confusion! From the beginning I have held this humanity as my greatest enemy; it has always filled me with intolerahle abhorrence. O men, so favored and gifted by your God. whom I abhor, and so ardently loved by Him! How shall I hinder your good fortune? How shall I bring upon you my unhappiness, since I cannot destroy the existence you have received? What shall we now begin, O my followers? How shall we restore our reign? How shall we recover our power over men? How shaH we overcome them? For if men from now on shall not be most senseless and ungrateful, if they are not worse <lisposed than we ourselves toward this God-man, who has redeemed them with so much love, it is clear that all of them will eagerly follow Him; none will take notice of our deceits; they will abhor the honors which we insidiously offer them, and will love contempt; they will seek the mortification of the flesh and will discover the danger of carnal pleasure and ease; they will despise riches and treasures, and love the poverty so much honored by their Master; and all that we can offer to their appetites they will abhor in imitation of their true Redeemer. Thus will our reign be destroyed, since no one will be added to our number in this place of confusion and torments; all will reach the happiness which we have

lost, all will humiliate themselves to the dust and suffer with patience; and my wrath and haughtiness will avail me nothing."

"Ah, woe is me, what torment does this mistake cause me! When I tempted Him in the desert, the only result was to afford Him a chance to leave the example of this victory, by following which men can overcome me so much the more easily. My persecutions only brought out more clearly his doctrine of humility and patience. In persuading Judas to betray Him, and the Jews to subject Him to the deadly torture of the Cross, I merely hastened my ruin and the salvation of men, while the doctrine I sought to blot out was only the more firmly implanted. How could One who is God humiliate Himself to such an extent? How could He bear so much from men who are evil? How could I myself have been led to assist so much in making this salvation so copious and wonderful? O how godlike is the power of that Man which could torment and weaken me so? And how can this Woman, his Mother and my Enemy, be so mighty and invincible in her opposition to me? New is such power in a mere creature, and no doubt She derived it from the divine Word, whom She clothed in human flesh. Through this Woman the Almighty has ceaselessly waged war against me, though I have hated Her in my pride from the moment I recognized Her in her image or heavenly sign. But if my proud indignation is not to he assuaged, I benefit nothing by my perpetual war against this Redeemer, against his Mother and against men. Now then, ye demons who follow me, now is the time to give way to our wrath against God. Come all of ye to take counsel what we are to do; for I desire to hear your opinions."

Some of the principal demons gave their answers to this dreadful proposal, encouraging Lucifer by suggesting diverse schemes for hindering the fruit 'of the Redemption among men. They all agreed that it was not possible to injure the person of Christ, to diminish the immense value of his merits, to destroy the efficacy of the Sacraments, to falsify or abolish the doctrine which Christ had preached; yet they resolved that, in accordance with the new order of assistance and favor established by God for the salvation of men, they should now seek new ways of hindering and preventing the work of God by so much the greater deceits and temptations. In reference to these plans some of the astute and malicious demons said: "It is true, that men now have at their disposal a new and very powerful doctrine and law, new and efficacious Sacraments, a new Model and Instructor of virtues, a powerful Intercessor and Advocate in this Woman; yet the natural inclinations and passions of the flesh remain just the same, and the sensible and delectable creatures have not changed their nature, Let us then, making use of this situation with increased astuteness, foil as far as in us lies the effects of what this God-man has wrought for men. Let us begin strenuous warfare against mankind by suggesting new attractions, exciting them to follow their passions in forgetfulness of all else. Thus men, being taken up with these dangerous things, cannot attend to the contrary."

Acting upon this counsel they redistributed the spheres of work among themseh'es, in order that each squadron of demons might, with a specialized astuteness, tempt men to different vices. They resolved to continue to propagate idolatry in the world, so that men might not come to the knowledge of the true God and the Redemption. Wherever idolatry would fail, they concluded to establish sects and heresies, for which they would select the most perverse and depraved of the human race as leaders and teachers of error. Then and there was concocted among these malignant spirits the sect of Mahomet, the heresies of Arius, Pelagius, Nestorius, and whatever other heresies have been started in the world from the first ages of the Church until now, together with those which they have in readiness, but which it is neither neces ary nor proper to mention here. Lucifer showed him~ !If content with these infernal counsels as being oppos d to divine truth and destructive of the very found;;tion of man's rescue, namely divine faith. He lavished flattering praise and high offices upon those demons, who showed themselves willing and who undertook to find the impious originators of these errors. Some of the devils charged themselves with perverting the inclinations of children at their conception and birth; others to induce parents to be negligent in the education and instruction of their children, either through an inordinate love or aversion, and to cause a hatred of parents among the children. Some offered to create hatred between husbands and wives, to place them in the way of adultery, or to think little of the fidelity promised to their conjugal partners. All agreed to sow among men the seeds of discord, hatred and vengeance, proud and sensual thoughts, desire of riches or honors, and by suggesting sophistical reasons against all the virtues Christ has taught; above all they intended to weaken the remembrance of his Passion and Death. of the means of salvation, and of the eternal pains of hell. By these means the demons hoped to burden all the powers and the faculties of men with solicitude for earthly affairs and sensual pleasures, leaving them little time for spiritual thoughts and their own salvation.

Lucifer heard these different suggestions of the demons, and answering them, he said: "I am much beholden to you for your opinions: I approve of them and adopt them all; it will be easy to put them into practice with those, who do not profess the law given by this Redeemer to men, though with those who accept and embrace these laws, it will be a difficult enterprise. But against this law and against those that follow it, I intend to direct all my wrath and fury and I shall most bitterly persecute those who hear the doctrine of this Redeemer and become his disciples; against these must our most relentless battle be waged to the end of the world. In this new Church I must strive to sow my cockle (Matthew 14, 25), the ambitions, the avarice, the sensuality, and the deadly hatreds, with all the other vices, of which I am the head. For if once these sins multiply and increase among the faithful, they will, with their concomitant malice and ingratitude, Irritate God and justly deprive men of the helps of grace left to them by the merits of the Redeemer. If once they have thus despoiled themselves of these means of salvation, we shall have assured victory over them. We must also exert ourselves to weaken piety and all that is spiritual and divine; so that they do not realize the power of the Sacraments and receive them in mortal sin, or at least without fervor and devotion. For since these Sacraments are spiritual, it is necessary to receive them with welldisposed will, in order to reap their fruits. If once they despise the medicine, they shall languish in their sickness and be less able to withstand our temptations; they will not see through our deceits, they will let the memory of their Redeemer and of the intercession of his Mother slip from their minds. Thus will their foul ingratitude make them unworthy of grace and so irritate their God and Savior, as to deprive them of his helps. In all this I wish, that all of you assist me strenuously, losing neither time nor occasion for executing my commands."

It is not possible to rehearse all the schemes of this dragon and his allies concocted at that time against the holy Church and her children, in order that these waters of Jordan might be swallowed up in his throat (Job 40, 18). It is enough to state that they spent nearly a full year after the Death of Christ in conferring and considering among themselves the state of the world up to that time and the changes wrought by Christ our God and Master through his Death and after having manifested the light of his faith by so many miracles, blessings and examples of holy men. If all these labors have not sufficed to draw all men to the way of salvation, it can be easily understood, that Lucifer should have prevailed and that his wrath should be so great, as to cause us justly to say with saint John: "Woe to the earth, for satan is come down to you full of wrath and fury!" But alas! that truths so infallible and so much to be dreaded and avoided by men, should in our days be blotted from the minds of mortals to the irreparable danger of the whole world! Our enemy is astute, cruel and watchful: we sleepy, lukewarm and careless! What wonder that Lucifer has intrenched himself so firmly in the world, when so many listen to him, accept and follow his deceits, so few resist him, and entirely forget the eternal death. which he so furiously and maliciously seeks to draw upon them? I beseech those, who read this, not to forget this dreadful <langer. If they are not convinced· of this danger through the evil condition of the world and through the evils each one experiences himself, let them at least learn of this danger by the vast and powerful remedies and helps, which the Savior thought it necessary to leave behind in his Church. For He would not have provided sllch antidotes if our ailment and danger of eternal death were not so great and formidable.

Instruction, Which the Queen of Heaven Gave Me

My daughter, by divine enlightenment thou hast received a deep understanding of the glorious triumph of . my Son and Lord on the Cross over the demons and of their rout and vanquishment. But thou must re: member that thou art yet ignorant of much more than what thou knowest concerning these ineffable mysteries. For in mortal flesh the creature cannot comprehend them in their reality, and divine Providence reserves the full understanding of them as a reward of the saints in heaven and for the beatific vision, in which these myse teries will be comprehended clearly. This insight will also be given to the reprobate, to each one according to his degree, for their confusion and punishment at the end of their career. But what thou hast learned will suffice to apprise thee of the dangers of this mortal life and to enliven thy hope of overcoming thy enemies. I wish also to warn thee of the new wrath, which the dragon has conceived especially against thee for what thou hast written in this chapter. He has ceaselessly pursued thee with his wrath and has sought to hinder thee from writing my life, as thou hast experienced continually in this work. But now his haughty pride is incensed against thee especially, because thou hast revealed his humiliation, his crushing ruin at the Death of my most blessed Son, the condition in which it left him and the secret counsels for revenging himself upon the children of Adam and especially upon the members of the holy church. All this has excited and disturbed

him anew, seeing that these secrets will be revealed tc those yet ignorant of them. Thou wilt feel his wrath in the difficulties he will place in thy way, the temptations and persecutions thou hast already encountered. Therefore I warn thee to be wary and circumspect against the rabid fury and cruelty of thy enemy.

Thou art astonished, and justly, to see, on the one hand, the power of my Son's merits and of his Redemption, the ruin and weakness caused by the demons in men; and, on the other hand. to see the power of the devil lording it over the world in haughty presumption. Although the light given to thee in writing this history is equal to this astonishment, I wish to add still another point of information, in order that thou mayest guard thyself so much the more carefully against enemies so full of malice. It is certain, that when hell came to the full knowledge of the sacrament of the Incarnation and Redemption, and of the poverty, humility and lowliness of the birth of Jesus, of his life and miracles, ending in the mysterious Passion and Death, and of all the rest of his labors to draw men to Him, Lucifer and his demons were weakened and disabled and they saw that they could not tempt the faithful in the same way as the rest of men and as they ceaselessly desire to do. In the primitive Church this terror and fear of the baptized, and of the followers of Christ our Lord, continued many years; for the divine virtues shone forth brightly in their imitation of Christ, in their zeal in confessing the faith, in following the teachings of the Gospel, in practicing heroic virtues and most fervent love, humility, patience and contempt of the vanities and deceits of the world. Many shed their blood and gave their life for Christ the Lord; they perfonned many admirable and exalted deeds for the glory of his name. This invincible fortitude resulted from their living at a time so near to the Passion and Death of their Redeemer and so close to the prodigious example of his patience and humility; but also because they were less tempted by the devils, who could not so soon rise from the crushing defeat brought upon them by the triumph of the crucified God.

This close imitation and living reproduction of Christ, confronting the demons in the first children of the Church, they feared so much, that they dared not approach and they precipitously fled from the Apostles and the just ones imbued with the doctrines of my divine Son. In them were offered up to the Almighty the first fruits of grace, and of Redemption. 'What is seen in the saints and in perfect

Christians in those times, would happen in the present times with all the Catholics if they would accept grace and work with it instead of permitting it to go to waste, and if they would seek the way of the Cross; for Lucifer fears it just as much now as in the times thou hast been writing of. But soon the charity, zeal and devotion in many of the faithful began to grow cold and they forgot the blessings of the Redemption; they yielded to their carnal inclinations and desires, they loved vanity and avarice, and permitted themselves to be fascinated and deceived by the false pretenses of Lucifer, obscuring the glory of their Savior and inveigling them into the meshes of their mortal enemies. This foul ingratitude has thrown the world into the present state and has encouraged the demons to rise up in their pride against God, audaciously presuming to possess themselves of all the children of Adam on account of this forgetfulness and carelessness of Catholics. They presume to plot the destruction of the whole Church by the perversion of so many who have fallen away from it; and by inducing those who are in it, to think little of it, or by hindering them from producing the fruits of the blood and death of their Redeemer. The greatest misfortune is, that many Catholics fail to recognize this great damage and do not seriJusly think of a remedy, although they can presume that the times, of which Jesus forewarned the women of Jerusalem, have arrived; namely, those in which the sterile should be happy, and in which many would call upon the mountains and the hills to cover and fall upon them, in order not to see the devastation of wickedness cutting down the sons of perdition, the dried trees, barren of ill the fruits of virtue. In these evil times dost thou live, my dearest; and in order that thou mayest not be included in the perdition of so many souls, do thou bewail it in the bitterness of thy heart, never forgetting the mysteries of the Incarnation, Passion and Death of my Divine Son. I desire thee to give thanks in compensation for the great number of those, who forget it, and I assure thee that the mere memory and contemplation of these mysteries are terrible to hell, torment and drive away the demons, and that they avoid and fly those who thankfully remember the life and passion of my divine Son.

The Side of Christ Is Opened With a Lance

As His Body is taken down, He is take down and buried, the Dogins of the Blessed Mother on this occasion, and until she returned to the cenacle.

The Evangelist saint John tells us that near the Cross stood Mary, the most holy !IIother of Jesus, with Mary Cleophas and Mary Magdalen. Although this is said of the time before Jesus expired, it must be understood, that the unconquerable Queen remained also afterwards, always standing beneath the Cross and adoring her dead Jesus and his divinity inseparably united to his sacred body. Amid the impetuous floods of sorrow, that penetrated to the inmost recesses of her chastest heart, the great Lady remained immovably constant in the exercise of ineffable virtues, while contemplating within Her the mysteries of man's Redemption and the order in which divine Wisdom disposed of all these sacraments. The greatest affliction of the Mother of mercy was the traitorous ingratitude, which men, to their own great loss, would show toward this extraordinary blessing, so worthy of eternal thanksgiving. But now She was especially solicitous for the burial of the sacred body of her divine Son and how to procure some one to take it down from the Cross. Full of this sorrowful anxiety, keeping her heavenly eyes riveted upon it, She turned to her holy angels around Her and spoke to them: "Ministers of the Most High, my friends in tribulation, you know that there is no sorrow like unto my sorrow; tell me then, how shall I take down from the Cross, whom my soul loves; how and where shall I give Him honorable burial, since this duty pertains to me as his Mother? Tell me what to do, and assist me on this occasion by your diligence."

The holy angels arrswered: "Our Queen and Mistress, let thy afflicted heart be dilated for what is still to be borne. The omnipotent Lord has concealed his glory and power from mortals in order to subject Himself to the cruelty of man's impious malice and has always permitted the laws established for the course of human events to be fulfilled. One of them is, that the condemned shall not leave the cross without the consent of the judge. We are ready and able to obey Thee and to defend our true God and Creator, but his wiII restrains us, because He wishes to justify his cause to the end and to shed the rest of the blood still in Him for the benefit of mankind and in order that He may bind them still more firmly to make a return for his copious and redeeming love (Psalms 79, 7). If they do not avail themselves of this blessing as they ought, their punishment shall be deplorable and its severity shall make amends for the longsuffering of God in delaying his vengeance." This answer of the angels increased the sorrow of the afflicted Mother; for it had not been as yet revealed to Her, that her divine Son should be wounded by the lance, and the fear of what should happen to the sacred body renewed her tribulation and anxiety.

She soon saw an armed band approaching Calvary; and in her dread of some new outrage against the deceased Savior, She spoke to saint John and the pious women: "Alas, now shall my affliction reach its utmost and transfix my heart! Is it possible, that the executioners and the Jews are not yet satisfied with having put to death my Son and Lord? Shall they now heap more injury upon his dead body?" It was the evening of the great Sabbath of the Jews, and in order to celebrate it with unburdened minds, they had asked Pilate for permission to shatter the limbs of the three men sentenced, so that, their death being hastened, they might be taken from the crosses and not left on them for the following day. With this intent the company of soldiers, which Mary now saw, had come to mount Calvary. As they perceived the two thieves still alive, they broke their limbs and so hastened their end (John 19, 31). But when they examined Jesus they found Him already dead, and therefore did not break his bones, thus fulfilling the mysterious prophecy in Exodus (Exodus 12, 46), commanding that no bones be broken in the figurative lamb to be eaten for the Pasch. But a soldier, by the name of Longinus, approaching the Cross of Christ, thrust his lance through the side of the Savior. Immediately water and blood flowed from the wound, as saint John, who saw it and who gives testimony of the truth, assures us (John 19, 34).

This wounding of the lance, which could not be felt by the sacred and dead body of the Lord, was felt by the most blessed Mother in his stead and in the same manner as if her chaste bosom had been pierced. But even this pain was exceeded by the affliction of her most holy soul, in witnessing the cruel laceration of the breast of her dead Son. At the same time, moved by compassion and love and in forgetfulness of her own sorrow, She said to Longinus: "The Almighty look upon thee with eyes of mercy for the pain thou hast caused to my soul!" So far and no farther went her indignation (or more properly, her most merciful meekness), for the instruction of all of us who are ever injured. For to the mind of this sincerest Dove, this injury to the dead Christ weighed most heavily; and the retribution sought by Her for the delinquent was one of the greatest blessings, namely that God should look upon him with eyes of mercy and return blessings and gifts of grace for the offense. Thus it also happened; for the Savior, moved by the prayer of his blessed Mother, ordained that some of the blood and water from his sacred side should drop upon the face of Longinus and restore to him his eyesight, which he had almost lost. At the same time sight was given to his soul, so that he recognized in the Crucified his Savior, whom he had so inhumanly mutilated. Through this enlightenment Longinus was converted; weeping over his sins and having washed them in the blood and water of the side of Christ, he openly acknowledged and confessed Him as the true God and Savior of the world. He proclaimed Him as such in the presence of the Jews, confounding by his testimony their perfidy and hardness of heart.

729. The most prudent Queen then perceived the mystery of this lance thrust, namely, that in this last pouring forth of the blood and water issued forth the new Church, cleansed and washed by the Passion and Death of Jesus, and that from his sacred side, as from the roots, should now spread out through the whole world the fruits of life eternal. She conferred within Herself also upon the mystery of that rock struck by the rod of divine justice (Exodus 17, 6), in order that the living waters might issue forth, quenching the thirst of all the human race and recreating and refreshing all who betook themselves to drink therefrom. She considered the coincidence of the five fountains from the wounds of his hands, feet and sides, which opened up the new paradise of the most holy humanity of our Savior, and which were more copious and powerful to fertilize the earth than those of the terrestrial paradise divided into four streams over the surface of the globe (Genesis 2, 10). These and other mysteries the great Lady rehearsed in a canticle of praise, which She composed in honor of her divine Son after his being wounded by the lance. Together with this canticle She poured forth a most fervent prayer, that all these mysteries of the Redemption be verified in the blessings spread over the whole human race.

The evening of that day of the parasceve was already approaching, and the loving Mother had as yet no solution of the difficulty of the burial of her dead Son, which She desired so much; but the Lord ordained, that the tribulations of his tenderest Mother should be relieved by Joseph of Arimathea and Nikodemus, whom he had inspired with the thought of caring for the burial of their Master. They were both just men and disciples of the Lord, although not of the seventytwo; for they had not as yet openly confessed themselves as disciples for fear of the Jews, who suspected and hated as enemies all those that followed Christ and acknowledged Him as Teacher. The dispositions of divine Providence concerning the burial of her Son had not been made known to the most prudent Virgin and thus her painful anxiety increased to such an extent, that She saw no way out of the difficulty. In her affliction She raised her eyes to heaven and said: "Eternal Father and my Lord, by the condescension of thy goodness and infinite wisdom I was raised to the exalted dignity of being the Mother of thy Son; and by that same bounty of an immense God Thou hast permitted me to nurse Him at my breast, nourish Him and accompany Him to his death. Now it behooves me as his Mother to give honorable burial to his sacred body, though I can go no farther than to desire it and deeply grieve, because I am unable to fulfill my wishes. I beseech thy divine Majesty to provide some way for accomplishing my desires."

This prayer the loving Mother offered up after the sacred body of the Lord was perforated by the lance. Soon after She saw another group of men coming toward Calvary with ladders and other apparatus seemingly for the purpose of taking from the Cross her priceless Treasure; but as She did not know their intentions, She was tortured by new fears of the cruelty of the Jews, and turning to saint John, She said: "My Son, what may be the object of these people in coming with all these instruments?" The apostle answered: "Do not fear them that are coming, my Lady; for they are Joseph and Nikodemus with some of their servants, all of them friends and servants of thy divine Son and my Lord." Joseph was just in the eyes of the Most High (John 19, 38), a noble decurion in the employment of the government, a member of the council, who as is given us to understand in the Gospel, had not consented to the resolves and the proceedings of the murderers of Christ and who had recognized Jesus as the true Messias. Although Joseph had been a secret disciple of the Lord, yet at his death, in consequence of the efficacious influence of the Redemption, he openly confessed his adherence. Setting aside all fear of the envy of the Jews and caring nothing for the power of the Romans, he went boldly to Pilate and asked for the body of Jesus (Mark 15, 43), in order to take Him down from the Cross and give Him honorable burial. He openly maintained that he was innocent and the true Son of God, as witnessed by the miracles of his life and death.

Pilate dared not refuse the request of Joseph, hut gave him full permission to dispose of the dead body of Jesus as he thought fit. With this permission Joseph left the house of the judge and called upon Nikodemus. He too was a just man, learned in divine and human letters and in the holy Scriptures, as is evident in what saint John related of him when he visited Christ at Night in order to hear the doctrine of Jesus Christ (John 3, 2). Joseph provided the winding sheets and burial cloths for the body of Jesus, while Nikodemus bought about one hundred pounds of the spices, which the Jews were accustomed to use in the burial of distinguished men (Matthew 27, 59). Provided with these and with other necessaries they took their way to Calvary. They were accompanied by their servants and some other pious and devout persons, in whom likewise the blood shed for all by the crucified God had produced its salutary effects.

They approached most Holy Mary, who, in the company of saint John and the holy women, stood in inconceivable sorrow at the foot of the Cross. Instead of a salute, their sorrow at the sight of so painful a spectacle as that of the divine Crucified, was roused to such vehemence and bitterness, that Joseph and Nikodemus remained for a time prostrate at the feet of the Queen and all of them at the foot of the Cross without speaking a word. All of them wept and sighed most bitterly until the invincible Queen raised them from the ground and animated and consoled them; whereupon they saluted Her in humble compassion. The most observant Mother thanked them kindly, especially for the service they were about to render to their God and Savior, and promised them the reward in the name of Him whose body they were to lay in the tomb. Joseph of Arimathea answered: "Even now, our Lady, do we feel in the secret of our hearts the sweet delight of the divine Spirit, who has moved us to such love, that we never could merit it or succeed in explaining it." Then they divested themselves of their mantles and with their own hands Joseph and Nikodemus placed the ladders to the holy Cross. On these they ascended in order to detach the sacred body, while the glorious Mother stood closely by leaning on the arms of saint John and Mary Magdalen. It seemed to Joseph, that the sorrow of the heavenly Lady would be renewed, when the sacred body should be lowered and She should touch it, and therefore He advised the Apostle to take Her aside in order to draw away her attention. But saint John, who knew better the invincible heart of the Queen, answered that from the beginning She had stood by to witness the torments of the Lord and that She would not leave him whom She venerated as her God and loved as the Son of her Womb.

Nevertheless they continued to urge the expediency of her retiring for a short time, until they should lower their Master from the Cross. But the great Lady responded: "My dearest masters, since I was present, when my sweetest Son was nailed to the Cross, fear not to allow me to be present at his taking down; for this act of piety, though it shall affect my heart with new sorrow, will, in its very performance, afford a great relief." Thereupon they began to arrange for the taking down of the body. First they detached the crown from the head, laying bare the lacerations and deep wounds it had caused. They handed it down with great reverence and amid abundant tears, placing it in the hands of the sweetest Mother. She received it prostrate on her knees, in deepest adoration bathed it with her tears, permitting the sharp thorns to wound her virginal countenance in pressing it to her face. She asked the eternal Father to inspire due veneration toward the sacred thorns in those Christians, who should obtain possession of them in futt1re times.

In imitation of the Mother, saint John with the pious women and the other faithful there present, also adored it; and this they also did with the nails, handing them first to most holy Mary for veneration and afterward showing their own reverence. Then the great Lady placed Herself on her knees and held the unfolded cloth in her outstretched arms ready to receive the dead body of her Son. In order to assist Joseph and Nikodemus, saint John supported the head, and Mary Magdalen the feet, of Christ and thus they tearfully and reverently placed Him into the arms of his sweetest Mother. This was to Her an event of mixed sorrow and consolation; for in seeing Him thus wounded and all his beauty disfigured beyond all children of men (Psalms 44, 3), the sorrows of her most chaste heart were again renewed; and in holding Him in her anns and at her breast, her incomparable sorrow was rejoiced and her love satiated by the possession of her Treasure. She looked upon Him with supreme worship and reverence, shedding tears of blood. In union with Her, as He rested in her arms, all the multitude of her attendant angels worshipped Him, although unseen by all others except Mary. Then saint John first, and after him all those present in their turn, adored the sacred Body. The most prudent Mother, seated on the ground, in the meanwhile held Him in her arms In order that they might satisfy their devotion.

736. In all these proceedings our great Queen acted with such heavenly wisdom and prudence, that She excited the admiration of the angels and men; for all her words were full of the deepest significance, the most winning affection and compassion for her deceased Son, full of tenderness in her lamenting, and full of mystery in sentiment and meaning. Her sorrow exceeded all that could ever be felt by mortals. She moved the hearts to compassion and tears. She enlightened all in

the understanding of the sacrament now transpiring under their hands. Above all, without failing in the least of her duties, She preserved her humble dignity and serenity of countenance in the midst of her heartrending affliction. With uniform adaptation to the circumstances She spoke to her beloved Son, to the eternal Father, to the angels, to the bystanders, and to the whole human race, for whose Redemption the Lord had undergone his Passion and Death. I will not detain myself in particularizing the most prudent and sorrowful words of the Lady on this occasion; for Christian piety will be able to conceive many of them, and I cannot stay to enumerate all these mysteries.

Some time passed during which the sorrowful Mother held at her breast the dead Jesus, and as evening was far advancing, saint John and Joseph besought Her to allow the burial of her Son and God to proceed. The most prudent Mother yielded; and they now embalmed the sacred body, using all the hundred pounds of the spices and the aromatic ointments brought by Nikodemus. Thus anointed the deified body was placed on a bier, in order to be carried to the sepulchre. The heavenly Queen, most attentive in her zealous love, called from heaven many choirs of angels, who, together with those of her guard, should accompany the burial of their Creator. Immediately they descended from on high in shapes visible to their Queen and Lady, though not to the rest. A procession of heavenly spirits was formed and another of men, and the sacred body was borne along by saint John, Joseph, Nikodemus and the centurion, who had confessed the Lord and now assisted at his burial. They were followed by the blessed Mother, by Mary Magdalen and the rest of the women disciples. Besides these a large number of the faithful assisted, for many had been moved by the divine light and had come to Calvary after the lancethrust. All of them, in silence and in tears, joined the procession. They proceeded toward a nearby garden, where Joseph had hewn into the rock a new grave, in which nobody had as yet been buried or deposited (John 19,41). In this most blessed sepulchre they placed the sacred body of Jesus. Before they closed it up with the heavy stone, the devout and prudent Mother adored Christ anew, causing the admiration of men and angels. They imitated Her, all of them adoring the crucified Savior now resting in his grave; thereupon they closed the sepulchre with the stone, which, according to the Evangelist, was very heavy (Matthew 27,60).

At the same time the graves, which had opened at the Death of Christ, were again closed; for among other mysteries of their opening up, was this, that these graves as it were unsealed themselves in order to receive Him, whom the Jews had repudiated, when He was alive and their Benefactor. At the command of the Queen many angels remained to guard the sepulchre, where She had left her heart. In the same order and silence, in which they had come. they now returned to Calvary. The heavenly Mistress of an virtues approached the holy Cross and worshipped it in deepest reverence. In this Joseph and all the rest of the mourners followed Her. It was already late and the sun had sunk. when the great Lady betook Herself from Calvary to the house of the Cenacle in the company of the faithful. Having brought Her to the Cenacle. Saint John, the Marys and the others took leave of Her with many tears and sighs and asked for her benediction. The most humble and prudent Lady thanked them for their service to her divine Son and the consolation afforded Her; She permitted them to depart with many hidden and interior favors and with the blessing of her most amiable and kindest heart.

The Jews. confused and disturbed by the events. went to Pilate on the morning of the sabbath and asked him for soldiers to guard the sepulchre; for Christ. this seducer. they said. had openly announced. that after three days He would arise; hence his disciples might steal the body and then say that He had arisen. Pilate yielded to this malicious measure and gave them the guard they desired. which they stationed at the sepulchre (Matthew 28. 12). But the perfidious priests merely wished to palliate. the event. which they feared would really happen. as was manifest afterwards. when they bribed the soldiers of the guard to testify. that Jesus had not arisen. but had been stolen by the disciples. As no counsel will prevail against God (Proverbs 21. 30). the Resurrection of Christ became only so much the more public and was the more fully confirmed.

Instruction, Which the Queen of Heaven Gave Me

My daughter. the lance thrust which my blessed Son received in his side. was cruel and very painful only to me; but its effects and mysteries are most sweet to those souls who know how to taste its sweetness. It was a great affliction to me; but whoever meets with this mysterious favor will find it a great relief and consolation in his sorrows. In order that thou mayest understand this and participate in it, thou must know, that my Son and Lord, on account of his most ardent love for men, in addition to the wounds of the feet and hands, wished to open the wound of his heart, the seat of love, in order that through this port the souls might enter and there receive refuge and relief. This is the only retreat which I wish thee to seek during the time of thy banishment, and which thou must consider as thy habitation upon earth. There thou wilt find the conditions and laws of love for imitating me and learn how for injuries thou must return blessings to all who commit them against thee and thine, just as thou hast seen me do, when I was grieved by the wounding of the side of my dead Son. I assure thee, my dearest, that thou canst not do anything more adapted to the obtaining of the efficacious graces from the Almighty. The prayer, which thou offerest in a forgiving spirit, is powerful not only for thy own good, but for the good of the one that offends thee; for the kind heart of my Son is easily moved, when He sees that creatures imitate Him in pardoning offenders and in praying for them; for they thereby participate in his most ardent charity manifested on the Cross. Write this doctrine in thy heart and in imitation of me practice this virtue, of which I thought so highly. Through this wound look upon the heart of Christ thy Spouse and upon me, sweetly and ardently loving in it thy enemies and all creatures.

Consider also the anxious and ever ready providence of the Most High in coming to the aid of the creatures, that call to Him in true confidence. This thou hast seen in my behalf, when I found myself afflicted and at a loss concerning the proper burial of my divine Son. In order to come to my assistance in this plight, the Lord showed his sweet love by moving the hearts of Joseph and Nikodemus and of the other faithful to assist me in burying Him. By their opportune help I was so much consoled in this tribulation, that on account of their behavior and my prayer the Most High filled them with wonderful influences of the Divinity, by which they were regaled during the time of taking Jesus from the Cross and his burial; and from that time on these faithful were enlightened and filled with the mysteries of the Redemption. This is the admirable disposition of the sweet and powerful providence of God, that in order to bind Himself to do good to some of his creatures, He sends affliction upon others, thus giving an occasion for the practice of benevolence, so that at the same time those in necessity may be benefited. Thus the benefactor, on account of the good work he does and on account of the prayer of the poor, is rewarded by receiving graces of which he otherwise would not be worthy. The Father of mercies, who inspires and assists the good work done, afterwards pays for it as if it were due in justice. For we can correspond to his inspirations merely according to our insignificant abilities, while all that is really good, comes entirely from his hands (James 1, 17).

Consider also the equity maintained by this Providence in compensating the injuries received in patient suffering. For after my divine Son had suffered death amid the contempt, dishonor and blasphemies of men, the Most High at once provided for an honorable burial and moved many to confess Him as the true God and Redeemer, to proclaim Him as holy, innocent and just, and, at the very time when they had finished their frightful crucifixion, to adore Him as the Son of God. Even his enemies were made to feel within themselves the horror and confusion of their sin in persecuting Him. Although these benefits availed not all men, yet all of them were effects of the innocent Death of the Lord. I also concurred in my prayers, in order that the Lord might be acknowledged and honored by those known to me.

For more wonderful Traditional Catholic Books Go to:

christthekinglibrary.com

Made in the USA
Columbia, SC
15 April 2025

56672156R00091